School Leadership That Works

School Leadership That Works

Ideas from Around the World

Edited by Peter R. Litchka

ROWMAN & LITTLEFIELD
Lanham • Boulder • New York • London

Published by Rowman & Littlefield
An imprint of The Rowman & Littlefield Publishing Group, Inc.
4501 Forbes Boulevard, Suite 200, Lanham, Maryland 20706
www.rowman.com

6 Tinworth Street, London SE11 5AL

Copyright © 2019 by Peter R. Litchka

All rights reserved. No part of this book may be reproduced in any form or by any electronic or mechanical means, including information storage and retrieval systems, without written permission from the publisher, except by a reviewer who may quote passages in a review.

British Library Cataloguing in Publication Information Available

Library of Congress Cataloging-in-Publication Data Available

ISBN 978-1-4758-4106-0 (cloth : alk. paper)
ISBN 978-1-4758-4107-7 (pbk. : alk. paper)
ISBN 978-1-4758-4108-4 (electronic)

To my first grandchild, Ethan. The future is yours. *Carpe Diem*.

Contents

Acknowledgements ix

Introduction 1
    Peter R. Litchka

1 What Matters Most in the Design of Universal Professional Learning for School Leaders: An International Perspective   5
    Matt Byrne, Andy Scott, Carol Caverley, and Liz Wenden

2 Preparation of School Leaders in China: Past to Present Practices   31
    Tak Cheung Chan, Zhiding Shu, and Dehua Liu

3 Complex Adaptive Leadership for School Principals (CAL-SP): Theory and Practice in the Case of Turkish Schools   47
    Hamit Özen and Selahattin Turan

4 Developing Great Educational Leaders: The Ontario College Experience   71
    David A. Veres and Holly Catalfamo

About the Authors   91

About the Editor   93

Acknowledgements

I would like to thank the International Society for Educational Planning (ISEP), of which I have been a member since 2006. ISEP has a commitment to healthy and pertinent discourse regarding education, and this commitment first and foremost is of a global nature. Without ISEP, I doubt I would have not only been able to travel to countries such as Cyprus, Hungary, Israel, Poland, and Turkey, but of more importance, I would not have been able to meet educators from these and other countries in a professional and collegial manner. And thank you to Walter Polka, my friend and mentor, who encouraged me to join ISEP back in 2006.

I wish to thank Loyola University Maryland, particularly Joshua Smith, the dean of the School of Education. Loyola has provided me with much support and encouragement to continue my scholarship, including a sabbatical to complete the book! In addition, I recognize Mickey Fenzel of Loyola, for his friendship, mentoring, and guidance.

I would like to thank Stephanie Dunford for her keen editorial sense and critique in the development of this book. Her insights, questions, critiques and reviews were most helpful.

I wish to express my gratitude to Emine from Turkey, Orly from Israel, and Rafał from Poland for not only opening their homes to me, but for showing me the beauty of their countries and introducing me to some of the friendliest and interesting people I have ever been around.

Finally, I cannot end without acknowledging my wife, Isabella, for her support and faith in me. Without her, this book never happens!

Introduction

Peter R. Litchka

The Bridge Builder

An old man going a lone highway,
Came, at the evening cold and gray,
To a chasm vast and deep and wide.
Through which was flowing a sullen tide
The old man crossed in the twilight dim,
The sullen stream had no fear for him;
But he turned when safe on the other side
And built a bridge to span the tide.

Old man, said a fellow pilgrim near,
You are wasting your strength with building here;
Your journey will end with the ending day,
You never again will pass this way;
You've crossed the chasm, deep and wide,
Why build this bridge at evening tide?

The builder lifted his old gray head;
Good friend, in the path I have come, he said,
There followed after me to-day
A youth whose feet must pass this way.
This chasm that has been as naught to me
To that fair-haired youth may a pitfall be;
He, too, must cross in the twilight dim;
Good friend, I am building this bridge for him!

—Will Allen Dromgoole (1860–1934)

About one thousand feet north of the American Falls sits the iconic Rainbow Bridge, connecting Niagara Falls, New York (United States) with Niagara

Falls, Ontario (Canada). The bridge is approximately 950 feet long, more than two hundred feet above the raging waters of the Niagara River, and is used by more than four million people each year—either by car or by foot—to cross back and forth between these two countries.

Growing up in Niagara Falls, New York, my family and I would often cross the Rainbow Bridge to visit Canada. Traversing the bridge provides a stunning view of both the Canadian Horseshoe Falls and the American Falls. I have always been amazed at the different types of people from around the world that were using this bridge. How more robust, particularly from a cultural perspective, both Niagara Falls, Ontario and Niagara Falls, New York and the surrounding areas had become because of the bridge.

While some like to build bridges, others like to build walls. Walls are the means to keep others out, reject new or different ideas and cultures, or to ensure a sense of security and superiority over others who may be different. Perhaps proponents of walls think that they and the culture they represent are superior to others. Or maybe they are scared of the idea that someone, who may not look like them, speak like them, or act like them, might have better ideas. Thus, a wall is the only way to ensure that this fear can be eliminated. Yet, all one needs to do is look back in history at the failure of walls to do what they were supposed to do.

Symbolically, bridges can be viewed in terms of:

- Overcoming obstacles
- Opportunities
- Transition
- Pathway
- Link from the past to the future
- Welcome
- From danger to safety
- Open arms

For those who wish to improve the education for all children around the world—teachers, scholars, government officials, policy makers, and school leaders—engaging with others can be critical to improving the craft of school leadership. But this engagement should not only be within their own region and nation, but from around the world. This free flow of information will not only help to improve the lives of all children within the global community, but will strengthen the world from within!

At no time in the modern era has there been a greater call for having schools with effective leaders at the helm. The literature is very clear as to the point regarding why school leadership matters—just as it does in government, private business, public entities, and other types of organizations and institutions.

Schools, whether they are high-performing or low-performing; rich with resources or faced with scare resources; located in urban, suburban, or rural areas; or financed with public or private funds, will not be able to carry out their mission in terms of improving student achievement if there is not an effective leader at the helm. This is not to say that there is a specific theory or practice that every principal in every school throughout the world must follow. Culture certainly plays a significant role of how leadership is perceived and carried out, including but not limited to what the words *school leader* may mean from one country to another, one region of the world to another.

To have this discussion is not necessarily a novel idea. Considering the world today, in which we see the rise of despots and increasing nationalism occurring, it is timely that those of us in the field of educational leadership, from wherever we are, to reaffirm the notion that listening, sharing, and interacting with others from around the world can make the world a better place. It is my hope that this book can provide a spark of interest, a reaffirmation, or a building block for what can be accomplished through sharing global scholarship within the field of educational leadership. And by being "bridge builders," as described by Dromgoole.

* * * *

Over the past two decades, I have had the opportunity to visit and complete scholarship in nations such as Canada, Cyprus, Israel, Poland, and Turkey, as well as my native country of the United States. During my travels, I have learned much about these other nations, their people, and of course, their educational systems. But most of all, I have learned that listening is much better than speaking. And I learned it the hard way.

While making at a presentation at a university in Europe, one professor stood up during my presentation and said to me, "Why is it you Americans always speak to us as if you know everything and we know nothing!" And I did not, at that moment, have an answer. But the incident gave me great pause to think and reflect.

The genesis of this book came about while I was attending the annual conference of the International Society for Educational Planning (ISEP) in October 2017 in Toronto, Canada. As a member of this organization since 2006 and its current president, I have had the opportunity to listen to so many presentations from around the world—east and west, north and south. A persistent theme of these conference presentations was that, regardless of what part of the world the presenter was from, successes abound, particularly in the field of educational leadership. It was in Toronto that the idea came to me, why not put a book together of a series of scholarly articles that reflect these successes and challenges, in the hope that we can actually learn from each other, so that educational leaders around the world can add to their "toolboxes"?

* * * *

For this book, four chapters are presented, and each focuses on preparing future school leaders and supporting current school leaders. This includes a multinational approach to universal school-leadership development, an overview of past and present school-leadership development in China, an examination from Turkey of leadership in terms of the nature of interactions within a school between the leader and others, and a perspective on the development of educational leaders within the postsecondary context in Ontario, Canada.

* * * *

Perhaps a more succinct way to view this book is that school leadership continues to evolve as this position becomes more and more important in *every school in the world!* There is no one right way to lead, but there are many ways to for us to consider, to try, to modify, to grow, and to evolve. Children everywhere throughout the world need and deserve great schools, great teachers, and great school leaders.

It is my hope that readers will not only come away with new ideas and concepts of interest in the field of school leadership, but, regardless of where we live in this world—can *and* will:

- Reflect upon our own leadership in terms of learning and professional growth;
- Develop a deeper understanding one's own preference, dispositions, and biases in terms of how we each view school leadership;
- Develop a better understanding and appreciation of how school leadership is viewed in other cultures;
- Provide more opportunities for communication and collaboration across cultures—particularly across cultures that are different than one's own.

Editor's note: The use of the word *principal* and the words *school leader[ship]* will be used interchangeably throughout the book, unless otherwise noted.

Chapter One

What Matters Most in the Design of Universal Professional Learning for School Leaders

An International Perspective

Matt Byrne, Andy Scott,
Carol Caverley, and Liz Wenden

ACKNOWLEDGEMENT

We would like to thank the organizations and school leaders who participated in this inquiry. Their collective passion for improving school leadership has been inspiring!

INTRODUCTION

Our international, collaborative inquiry set out to explore and advance our understanding of how to develop the practices of school leaders in different cultures. In particular, we explore "what matters most" in designing professional learning for school leaders and advancing a set of universal design principles.

In advancing our understanding, we investigated the impact of the International School Leadership Certificate Program (ISLCP), one program that purports to be universal and is delivered in a wide array of jurisdictions around the world. For our purposes, we selected three of these jurisdictions to explore these key questions: What theories, concepts, and research presented in the program resulted in changing the leadership practices of the participants? What is required in the contextualization of a professional learning program that is designed to be universal? What universal design principles emerge?

The three case studies, including Scandinavia, the Caribbean, and Australia, provide rich stories of how the ISLCP impacted practice. In the end, the evidence supports the proposition that a professional learning certificate program for school leaders, designed according to key universal principles, is a powerful approach to enhance performance, regardless of local culture and context.

THE INTERNATIONAL SCHOOL LEADERSHIP CERTIFICATE PROGRAM

International School Leadership Ltd. delivers professional learning for school leaders around the world, with online, hybrid, and onsite delivery. The core program consists of six modules, equating to sixty hours of instruction (internationalschoolleadership.com).

The theories, concepts, and research presented in the program are intentionally selected to reflect an international perspective, although the Ontario, Canada experience is well represented (internationalschoolleadership.com). These resources constantly change as new ideas emerge and consultation across the globe occurs. Some changes in the program take place to align with district initiatives and related documents; however, the vast majority of the program remains the same from one region to another.

The program is designed for school leaders in various roles, ranging from principal to lead teacher, as well as system and governance roles. The program has been delivered to role-specific groups and to groups representing all of the aforementioned roles (internationalschoolleadership.com).

The program is recognized for credit within master's degrees offered by four universities in Hong Kong, Australia, and Canada. Furthermore, the content of the ISL program is embedded in a master's degree offered by one of these universities and represents 50 percent of the coursework.

WHAT WE KNOW TODAY

First, we know that the growing multidimensional demands on today's school leaders require a wider range of skills than those obtained in the course of a teaching degree or through generic professional development delivered to teachers throughout their teaching career. Today, school leaders are expected to exercise their own discretion in school, staff, and curriculum management, and bear the burden of many expectations relating to operational and academic accountability, instructional leadership, teacher quality, and school and student achievement; the list continues to grow.

However, the content of many professional development programs has not evolved to reflect these expectations (Asuga, Eacott, and Scevak, 2015; Clarke and Styles, 2011; Devin, 2016). In fact, the research paints an unflattering picture and demonstrates a need to refocus programs to address globally minded school-leadership development, to support the need for innovation, to respond to the rapid changes in societal culture, and to answer the need for a framework for best practice (Easley and Tulowitzki, 2013).

Next, we know that effective school leadership influences student learning and school improvement, second only to classroom instruction (Devin, 2016; Eacott, 2013; Ng, 2017). How school leaders are prepared for their roles is important (Asuga et al., 2015; Eacott, 2013; McCarthy, 2015; Ng, 2017).

We also know that even though the role of school leader continues to evolve and varies from one jurisdiction to another, common core competencies appear in leadership frameworks. For example, the use of data in school improvement efforts appeared as a set of practices in leadership frameworks. Other core competencies included setting direction (vision), building relationships, promoting collaboration, allocating resources, and building community connections (Ministry of Education 2012).

And finally, research has indicated that graduates of training programs that run in conjunction with universities are often more successful than programs facilitated by training providers alone. Using an approach that promoted partnerships between educational districts and universities and a merger of theory and practice positively impacted on graduates' acquisition of knowledge and engagement in effective leadership practices (Devin, 2016; Ng, 2017). These programs had a common set of characteristics (Devin, 2016; McCarthy, 2015; Ng, 2017; Piggot-Irvine and Youngs, 2011; Hallinger, Adams, Harris, and Jones, 2018):

- standards-based knowledge;
- coherent curriculum and philosophy emphasizing leadership of instruction and school improvement;
- supportive student principal cohorts for principals;
- rigorous candidate selection, including self-efficacy, emotional intelligence, autonomy, instructional skills, and knowledge; and
- knowledgeable faculty.

In addition, the aforementioned studies identified core program elements, such as an international curriculum, with specific elements linked to local context (Asuga et al., 2015) and the facility to undertake personal reflection to develop knowledge in and of principal practice (Easley and Tulowitzki, 2013; Piggot-Irvine and Youngs, 2011). Specifically, diverse curriculum embraced a wide range of expectations and accountabilities, including:

- learning for personal transformation;
- student-outcomes focus;
- evaluation and adaptation of initiatives in response to sector climate/needs;
- soft and hard skills;
- international and cross-cultural exposure;
- team work, including horizontal and vertical collaboration and distributed leadership;
- linking leadership development with organizational goals;
- use of multiple learning methods (Piggot-Irvine and Youngs 2011); and
- Use of a capstone project rather than dissertation or thesis (Hallinger et al., 2018; McCarthy, 2015).

Overall, research has provided a picture of the current state of professional learning programs for school leaders and a common understanding from which to explore the key questions of this study.

HOW IT WORKED: THE METHODOLOGY

In investigating what matters most in the design of universal professional learning for school leaders, the case study approach was used to provide insight into school leaders' perceptions of the ISL program across three international locations. A case study can be described as an in-depth and comprehensive study of a specific individual, group of individuals, or event. Case studies are used to explore the interactions between a phenomenon and the context in which it occurs (Pacho, 2015; Yin, 2014).

A total of twenty-five school leaders were involved in this study from three regions across the world including Scandinavia, the Caribbean, and Australia. The school leaders were purposefully selected as they had just participated in the ISL program and were interviewed to determine their perceptions of the ISL program and provide insight into the effectiveness of international professional learning for school leaders. The research was qualitative as it had a focus on the meaning of an experience to the participants in a natural setting and provided a descriptive, holistic account of this experience or phenomenon (Creswell, 2007b; Pacho, 2015).

Semistructured interviews were used to collect data. Each interview was approximately one hour in length and digitally recorded by the interviewer. All of the interviews in the Caribbean and Australia were conducted in person; several of the Scandinavian interviews were conducted online using a web conferencing service, while the majority took place in person. The questions were designed to probe school leaders' interaction and understanding of all of the program modules.

Case Studies

School leaders from the jurisdictions of Scandinavia, Caribbean, and Australia were interviewed for this study. In selecting the jurisdictions for the case studies, efforts were made to represent northern and southern hemispheres, as well as large and small jurisdictions. Furthermore, although the language of instruction is English, we wanted to include a jurisdiction where English was a second language.

The Scandinavian case study involved five school leaders including recently appointed principals and vice principals, a recently appointed system leader, and several seasoned principals. In the case of the Caribbean study, seven principals and deputies were involved in the study. And, finally, the Australian case study involved very seasoned principals, deputies, and recently appointed deputies.

Data Analysis Abridged

Each transcript was read and subjected to an initial coding process undertaken by one member of the research team. All transcripts were reread and coded according to a number of common key leadership themes. After this initial analysis, all members of the research team reviewed and refined the qualitative analysis and conducted a secondary check of the initial coding. From this secondary coding process, key leadership themes were identified for each international case, and these are detailed below.

This process also identified key leadership themes across each of the three cases that informed what matters most in terms of the professional learning of school leaders and, the design and delivery principles that should inform the delivery of international universal school leadership programs.

WHAT WAS FOUND

In Scandinavia

For the Scandinavian participants, five key leadership themes were identified by school leaders as making a difference in their practice: use of data, importance of being a lead learner, relationship building, walkthroughs, and assessment as learning.

What Did They Say About Using Data?

All Scandinavian participants reported on the revelation that data offers the potential to support a wide range of leadership practices intended to improve understanding, collective action, and overall learning. The revelation, however, was accompanied by a clearer understanding that collecting data "is a starting point for change" (Participant) and that using data effectively requires time, commitment, "a rich variety of information" (Participant), and a willingness to question past assumptions and beliefs. One principal summarized the change in practice this way:

> And so, we have used the data quite a lot . . . getting to know a school everyone thinks they know by heart and knows very well in a new way, because we have started to look at data over a larger span of time, or a certain span of time, and we have started to see that there are certain developments that it's important for us to work with that [we] haven't identified before. (Participant)

In fact, this more in-depth understanding of data enabled leaders to articulate to their communities that things are not always what they seem: "Here's some data that can show you this is not only a school problem, this is also maybe a community problem for this part of the municipality that we have to work together on" (Participant). For example, with effective data use, this principal was able to quell a parent and community concern about the school's marking system.

According to our research, successful use of data, such as this example, builds the leader's confidence and enthusiasm for using data. Equally important, however, is the leader's impact on collective inquiry practices within their school.

> We got into data and what it's really about with all the perspectives and all the things you observe and all the conversations you have. All the things that you know, making the whole picture. . . . They are inspired to continue to understand the power of data use. . . . our ultimate goal is to have the visible data and for me to go in and see that [name] has moved from there to there. (Participant)

Overall, participants reported significant improvement in their knowledge, confidence, and ability to use data effectively.

What Did They Say About the Importance of Being a Lead Learner?

In Scandinavia, the idea of becoming a lead learner was very compelling and widely accepted as a key leadership strategy. In the learning process, participants reflected on their practice and defined the idea in personal terms. For example, one participant defined the idea simply as: "To learn myself, to learn together with teachers, to plan for learning for the teachers, to set time and a place for it" (Participant). This understanding of the idea resulted in significant changes in practice: "I've been more focused on how to do learning processes in my own school, how to lead learning processes in staff meetings, etc. . . . and to be a part of the learning myself" (Participant).

Other participants also reported that they were more involved in getting to know what was happening in the classroom, such as the teaching practices and evidence of student learning. One participant provided a particularly powerful account of this change:

> [T]rying to be a support for my teachers in that respect. And that requires me to be where they are, in the classrooms, and being able to share my reflections on how the teaching is going in an open manner. Not to be a judge, but to be a partner, to reflect on teaching practices and how the students are involved in what's going on, and that is something that I am trying to do more of. (Participant)

Assuming the role of lead learner, although viewed as a laudable goal, was a major challenge. Leaders continued to struggle with balancing administrative tasks with learning tasks, but change was taking place.

> Since we attended these modules, I think we, at our school, we started working in a different way, or in a new way, little bit stronger focus on how to develop our school, not administratively, but in order to increase the quality of our teaching or the education for the students. (Participant)

Regardless of the challenges, the idea of lead learner changed their beliefs and assumptions about the role and, ultimately, changed their practice.

What Did They Say About Relationship Building?

At the outset, Scandinavian participants understood the significance of building strong relationships and trust as a basis for developing people. As one participant commented: "[I] understood that you need to be a people person. You need to understand other people. You need to motivate. It's about influence and not authority" (Participant). However, the deep focus on relationship-building strategies was reported as one of the most significant modules in the program. Indeed, participants described changes in beliefs, assumptions, and practices as a result of the learning.

> [W]e need to have people. You cannot do that alone. You are dependent on others, and my task, sort of, is to try and motivate and involve people so that we can have some shared ideas of what we need to do to make the school better. (Participant)

Clearly, the new learning reaffirmed fundamental beliefs about the importance of relationships while also refining leadership practices.

What Did They Say About Walkthroughs?

Scandinavian participants embraced walkthroughs as an efficient, effective way of finding out what was happening in the classroom and supporting teachers in their goal to improve teaching practices.

> I think to stay in a classroom for one hour is ineffective because I get so much information that I can't handle it afterward. I'm not able to give the teacher effective, good-quality feedback after I've stayed in a classroom for one hour . . . to scan the school by doing walkthroughs in my school is a nice way of get to know the school, get to know the teachers, get to know the needs of the teachers, the needs of the students. (Participant)

One principal, who enacted this basic practice, reported extending the use of walkthroughs to foster collaboration among teachers. In this case, after completing walkthroughs in multiple classrooms, the principal led a group discussion to provide collective feedback.

> It's interesting afterward, also, that I could give the group of teachers that I've just seen into a collective feedback. "I saw that when I was visiting your classroom." "I observed that you were going to . . . while I was observing that when I visited your classroom." "That was interesting. How come, or what have you planned before?" "Did it go the way that you planned for, or was it different when you were there as a teacher in the classroom?" "How come it was so different when you planned it together?" "Why did you plan it differently when you planned it together?" (Participant)

What Did They Say About Assessment as Learning?

In Scandinavia, the concept of assessment as learning resonated with the participants. Reportedly, leaders were interested in getting the students involved in their own assessment for the purposes of engagement and improved learning.

> This year we will concentrate on assessment and we will do assessment as learning and we will do these indicators, and only pick some of them. Then we can go deeper and we can see what we need to work on and just pick some of that, too. It's very small, and then if they want to, they can add more later. (Participant)

Regardless of the focus and effort, implementing practices for assessment as learning remained a challenge.

In the Caribbean

Caribbean participants identified walkthroughs, personal reflections, focus on student achievement, data use, and the concept of a learning organization as powerful ideas that change their practice.

What Did They Say About Walkthroughs?

Utilizing walkthroughs represented the most significant change in practice attributed to the program. In numerous cases, walkthroughs have been substituted for formal classroom observations.

> One thing I did bring in, which wasn't there before, was walkthroughs and learning walks, and the difference between doing a walkthrough and doing a formal observation. . . . We did tons of stuff with the walkthroughs. . . . The walkthrough stuff was probably the module we used for the project that we did implement here. The walkthrough was very influential. (Participant)

When using walkthroughs, the leaders in the Caribbean described how the focus of the visits shifted.

> Making it student-led, focus on the students themselves and what is happening in the classroom, rather than going there to be judgmental." (Participant)

And finally, walkthroughs were attributed to improvements in the collaborative nature of their relationship with teachers.

> It's made a huge difference because teachers, I think they embrace the suggestions that you give even more because they know that you're not there to judge them or to evaluate their practice. You're just there to have a look at what's going on and for help. (Participant)

What Did They Say About Personal Reflection?

Participants learned about the importance of reflecting on their new learning, experiences, and practices by doing it and having the engagement of others, including the instructor:

> It's extremely important to be able to self-reflect. . . . This particular module I find that made me really reflect a lot on myself. (Participant)

> The degree of collaboration, interaction within these groups was really good. (Participant)

What Did They Say About a Focus on the Student?

Participants offered many comments on the importance of focusing directly on the students and what they are doing in order drive change. Leaders accounted for shifts in their views and practices in efforts to directly support student learning. In fact, strategies were put in place to allow opportunities for students to think about their learning, reflect on their learning, set learning goals and empower themselves to learn.

> Seeing my teaching in the eyes, out of the eyes of that child, then that is going to impact how I plan instructions to cater to the needs of my kids. (Participant)

> The preparation, of course, but for children to be able to critically look at their work to say, "This is why it's good. What do I need to make better?" Of course, it's more effective feedback when they can give it to themselves. (Participant)

What Did They Say About Using Data?

Participants reported that collecting data was a common occurrence in all schools prior to the program. Furthermore, many claimed a good understanding of the importance of data for school improvement efforts.

> We are very good at, like I said, gathering information, but what are we actually doing it for? What are we using it for? How are we using it to move? What are we going to actually try to execute as a result of the data? (Participant)

> As a staff, we tend to know the data's there, but we're not really sure of how to look at it in terms of what the baseline is for students, and what the value added is. (Participant)

In fact, what the program provided for leaders was a deeper understanding of the uses of data and specific leadership strategies that could be used to maximize the impact.

> I definitely felt like we took away a lot more from the data aspect because we're gathering so much data currently, but we're not using that data. (Participant)

> I'm impressed with your data because one of the things I've never done or knew of is that data world. (Participant)

According to participants, the use of data strategies to drive educational decision making resulted in changes in teacher practice and school culture: "To actually use it, hard-core data, in order to inform practice, to put goals in place, get back to your school improvement plan, etc. It was very useful." (Participant)

What Did They Say About the Concept of a Learning Organization?

Participants in the Caribbean described the development of their thinking about learning organizations as opposed to traditional organizations. In addition, these leaders demonstrated a sound understanding of the concept by referring to different aspects of a learning organization when describing their school: "What we did together as a team, we looked at the broad school improvement plan, but we were able to come up with an action plan using that data to support our students" (Participant).

Another stated,

> We pulled a lot into our school with developing a growth mind set. (Participant)

> When you're a leader, you want to inspire others to be leaders, not to have a collection of followers. . . . We also encourage teachers that have the skills to be able to, not just myself, who is in a leadership position, but to conduct professional development in the staff meetings. So, inquiring as a whole. (Participant)

In Australia

Australian participants identified the following key areas of learning: embracing collaborative learning cultures, the importance of knowing the why, confidence, principal as lead learner, and the impact of data.

What Did They Say About Embracing the Idea of Collaborative Learning Cultures?

Every Australian participant commented about the need to increase collaboration among their staff and how what they learned in the program assisted in achieving this goal. Specifically, these leaders took positive action: "We set up collaborative learning groups and it was focused on the actual research cycle" (Participant). "They've got a lot to offer each other, and that's the empowering part about working together to solve problems about student learning" (Participant). "And that was really good because getting the teachers going around looking at what other teachers were doing, very, very powerful" (Participant). "The collaborative inquiry we're on our way to doing those sorts of things, creating that culture . . . you know, the data collection" (Participant).

These leaders also embraced professional learning communities as a structure that builds a trusting and collaborative culture with a clear focus on student achievement. "We've created professional learning communities we've got four of them, sent them off to team leaders, school improvement PL, it's four days, two days this term, two days next term with an action type research project attached" (Participant).

What Did They Say About the Importance of Knowing the Why?

Many Australian participants talked about the work of Simon Senek (2011) and the importance of "knowing and sharing your why—purpose and belief" (Participant). The participants summarized "knowing your why" as being able to articulate reasons for implementing changes in their school and explaining the need for the change. "If you can make people understand your why, and if your why is grounded in the understandings of leadership principles, people will follow you because they respect your why" (Participant).

Of course, to be impactful, describing one's why must include the need for collaboration, data use, empowerment, and dedication to students. "I've got better at that, explaining to them why the change is needed, showing them that path, you know, and when they can see the why, they're a lot more willing to partake" (Participant). "So, I guess, my plan's around embedding the practices in the school, so when people come to school, this is what [our school] does. And this is why we do it" (Participant). And as one participant concluded, "[I]f you're not passionate about what you're doing, your why . . . if you don't understand your why, then you might as well just stay in bed" (Participant).

What Did They Say About the Importance of Confidence—Believing in Yourself; Believing in Your Staff?

Many participants commented on how the program provided them with the knowledge, skills, and practices required to build even greater confidence as an instructional leader. Two participants nicely summarized the impact.

> [The course] gave me confidence, and permission. And, it gave me the eyes to see that that's where school leadership needed to go. . . . the leaders being the lead learners and being, you know, being able to walk into a classroom and you still know what's going on. You know, that's so, so important. And to have the confidence to address teachers—that means strategies to address situations where teachers perhaps are not doing their best, or they are doing their best, but they're not doing the best for the kids. (Participant)

The benefits, however, were not limited to just the leaders. Reportedly, this increase in personal confidence on the part of the leader also translated to a greater confidence among the staff themselves, allowing them the autonomy to make decisions, set direction, and assume ownership for their own learning. "I view everybody as proficient until they prove me otherwise. I was able to bring out their strengths and use them effectively within the school. It's more about working with what you've got and building their capacity" (Participant).

> Empowering people to look at kids, know them as people and know them really deeply, and then move through putting faces on data, all that kind of stuff, and moving them through that process is really important, but I don't see it as something that I can walk in and do very quickly. (Participant)

What Did They Say About the Importance of Being a Lead Learner?

In Australia, many participants reported some level of understanding of the concept prior to the program. "The impact of an effective school leader sets everything in place" (Participant). "You've got to be a leading learner, you've got to be seen to keep up and drag your staff with you" (Participant).

The program, nevertheless, provided participants with the confidence, resources, and leadership practices to assume the role of lead learner.

> Using some of the readings, and also the documentation from the modules, as a planning piece and putting it in front of staff who have to go through the processes bit by bit and break it down, and work through a structured process. (Participant)

What Did They Say About Using Data?

Participants discussed the importance of using data in their schools and how it has influenced the culture of their schools.

> Teacher efficacy, getting a better idea of the understanding of really knowing the kids deeply and knowing data, and then moving forward that way. All that sort of personal development stuff as well, understanding the type of leader that I could be and am, and working out where I need to improve, or strengthen, rather than improve. (Participant)

Participants also reported how changes in using data within the school addressed system-level issues.

> Because if we're on an improvement process, the data would reflect that and so, you know, they [Department of Education] can have all the data they want because if we're demonstrating that we're on an improvement process, you know, there's nothing to worry about them [Department of Education] having access to the data. (Participant)

WHAT MATTERS MOST

When investigating what matters most in the professional learning of school leaders, there are some universal themes that were identified by school leaders across all three international case studies. These themes provide some insight into both the key learnings that school leaders find most important in their professional learning and how this professional learning should be designed and implemented.

Given the important influence of effective school leadership on student learning and school improvement (Eacott 2013; Fuller, Young, and Baker 2010), this section will explore initially the key learnings that school leaders found most valuable in their professional development and will then focus on the design and delivery principles that should inform universal school-leadership programs.

What Matters Most: Professional Learning

The power of any professional learning endeavor is in how well the learning is translated into practice. When investigating the impact of professional learning on school leaders, it is important to be able to show evidence of how the professional learning has impacted the practice in their school (Asuga, Eacott, and Scevak 2015; Ng 2017).

The school leaders in the three case studies articulated the complexity of the job as a school leader and expressed, in varying degrees, the lack of quality preparation and training they received in their role. This is consistent with recent evidence that revealed that principals believe training programs do not match with the realities of leadership in modern schools (Devin 2016). On the contrary, the school leaders that participated in the ISL program were not only positive in relation to their learning in the program but were able to clearly articulate how they used this learning in the leading of their schools.

In the three international case studies detailed above, there were some shared key universal themes that school leaders identified as the most important in terms of the professional learning that impacted their practice in their schools. These were key leadership themes that were consistently identified by school leaders across each of the international case studies as most important.

Although the school leaders identified a range of issues relating to professional learning, three universal themes emerged from the case studies that represent the leadership issues that mattered the most to them: focus on students and everybody knowing they are learning; leading in and through relationships; and leading through data.

These universal themes do not act in isolation but are intricately interrelated in how they are applied by the school leaders in the complex and multidimensional context of their schools. Thus, in further illuminating these universal themes in the next section, the way in which they overlap and interrelate will be accentuated in an effort to show how the principals' key learnings from the ISL program match the realities of leadership in modern schools across the globe.

It Is About Students and Everybody Knowing They Are Learning

From each of the case studies it is evident that the ISL program activated school leaders into getting back into classrooms—in visiting and spending more time in classrooms and initiating more meaningful interactions with students and teachers. This increased, purposeful interaction through vehicles such as walkthroughs put the learning of students at the forefront, as one school leader commented:

> Trying to be a support for my teachers in that respect. And that requires me to be where they are, in the classrooms, and being able to share my reflections on how the teaching is going in an open manner. Not to be a judge, but to be a partner, to reflect on teaching practices and how the students are involved in what's going on, and that is something that I am trying to do more of. (Participant)

The focus on learning and student output is further illustrated by other school leaders in the Caribbean and Australia who said: "Making it student-led, focus on the students themselves and what is happening in the classroom" (Participant) and "empowering people to look at kids, know them as people and know them really deeply" (Participant). This focus on the learner afforded school leaders valuable insight into the student perspective. Purposeful interaction at the classroom level helped to build positive relationships with students and staff alike and provided important insight for school leaders into the quality of instruction of their staff (Easley and Tulowitzki 2013).

A key point was an active decision on behalf of school leaders to make themselves more available to students and teachers in their classrooms, as intimated in the following:

> I try to make use of myself. I sit down with the students and ask them what they're learning and the teachers know that and give them an immediate feedback afterward, just of what I saw. The assessment part is very important because that also goes into the data piece. (Participant)

This is a key outcome of training that brings about practical and proactive change (McCarthy, 2015; Onguko, Abdalla, and Webber, 2008).

Across each of the three case studies, school leaders were taking ownership of the learning in their school community and identifying themselves in the role of lead learner. As one school leader in Scandinavia stated,

> I've been more focused on how to do learning processes in my own school, how to lead learning processes in staff meetings, etc., to learn myself, to learn together with teachers, to plan for learning for teachers, to set time and a place for it. (Participant)

"You've got to be a leading learner, you've got to be seen to keep up and bring your staff with you," was a further comment from an Australian principal. A principal from the Caribbean summarized this in the following: "So a leader is not just being a dictator, but it's creating that collegial area to support and guide your follow colleagues. And they would be motivated to reach that vision with you."

The notion of being a lead leaner was linked to the importance of the learning organization and embracing collaborative learning cultures at the whole school level. A more collective, collegial, and whole-school strategic approach emanated from a focus on student learning and captures the essence of "everybody knowing that they are learning." The "everybody" was found to be critical in the need for increased collaboration of school staff to work together on improving the learning of students.

In the Australian case, a school leader identified that the "empowering part about working together to solve problems about student learning" (Participant) and power of "collaborative learning groups helped keep a focus on the action learning cycle" (Participant).

In the Caribbean, school leaders commented, "We're all working within the same system and we need to help each other and collaborate" (Participant) and "where people continually expand their capacity to create the results they truly desire, where new and expansive patterns of thinking are nurtured, where collective aspiration is set free, and where people are continually learning to see the whole together" (Participant).

It was clear from the three case studies that students and their learning should always be at the center of any learning enterprise. It follows that any professional learning for school leaders should have this as a key focus. The next universal theme identified in each of the case studies was related to more of the "how to" with reference to school leadership and, in part, facilitated a focus on student learning given it related to the importance of leading in and through relationship.

Leading in and Through Relationship: Importance of Developing People and Building Relationships

When identifying what mattered most in the professional learning of school leaders, participants across each of the three international case studies identified leading in and through relationship as most important. Of any of the key learnings described, the importance of developing people's skills and building relationships permeated most of the responses. This may in part be explained by leading in and through relationship as the most significant practical "how to" when it comes to school leadership. Two Scandinavian principals commented,

> I'm really into building relationships and the importance of relationships on every level throughout the school and throughout the systems to make people work together. Because we really need to trust each other before we can really develop anything that resonates with everyone. (Participant)
> When I kind of learned more and understood that you need to be a people person. You need to understand other people. You need to motivate. It's about influence and not authority. (Participant)

Leading in and through relationship is consistent with Piggot-Irvine and Youngs (2011) who highlighted the importance of school leadership training programs developing inter- and intrapersonal skills. Schaefer (2015) also asserted that connecting with others was one of the most effective ways one can lead.

Among the three case studies, there was an emphasis on the value of building trust, as outlined by one of the Australian principals.

> So, the behaviors of high trust leaders was really interesting. I think I exhibit a few of those, which it was just good to have them highlighted and it makes me just think about when I'm dealing with staff, and working with staff and, how it was coming through. (Participant)

The building of trust was found to support bringing staff together to collaborate around the ultimate goal of student success. As one principal from the Caribbean commented, "Develop that level of trust so we could collaborate more for the benefit of our kids. That's the ultimate goal: student success" (Participant).

This notion was echoed by an Australian principal who described the power of teachers learning from each other, "they've got a lot to offer each other, and that's the empowering part about working together to solve problems about student learning" (Participant). As seen earlier from one principal from Scandinavia, "we really need to trust each other before we can really develop anything that resonates with everyone" (Participant), highlighting the importance of a collaborative, whole-school approach to student learning.

There was also a sense of leading in and through relationships, empowering others to take leadership over student learning. As one principal commented, "When you're a leader, you want to inspire others to be leaders, not to have a collection of followers" (Participant). Another principal commented, "It's all about empowering others to become leaders" (Participant). For many principals, relational trust empowered the ownership of student learning by everybody, which in turn empowered decision making around quality learning from a more collaborative and targeted approach.

Positive relationships built upon trust helped bring staff together to collaborate on a whole school approach to student learning. This was found to support effective change in the schools, as supported by Schaefer (2015), who argued that good leaders are better able to support change and work with more-diverse teams.

Leading Through Data: Instruction Is the Leadership/Informed by Data/ Data Does the Leading

It was evident that the use of data to support learning and teaching also mattered most in the professional learning of school leaders for principals across the three case studies. Each case presented a strong exposition of the use of data to inform the learning enterprise within each school.

For a number of principals, a key issue was to help their teachers understand the importance of student data and to build capacity on how to use the data to support learning. As one school leader from the Caribbean described,

> The issue that we've had more than anything else is just getting teachers familiar with that data, and familiar with what it means if the students are going up a level, for example, and are they giving value added. . . . teachers are setting targets based on that. (Participant)

Further to this was the notion that many school leaders "took away a lot more from the data aspect because we're gathering so much data currently, but we're not using that data" (Participant).

Leading through data was found to be a further key mechanism to develop a focus on student learning and outcomes of school leaders, as one principal summarized:

> How do we inform them of where they are? What are the next steps? What can you do to move a step further? Have we, or are we providing the support these kids need? Because all kids are not the same. They learn at a different pace. They have different abilities. They have different needs. (Participant)

There was also agreement between the principals across the cases that data "is the starting point for change" (Participant) and "we get a rich variety of information we can base our decisions on" (Participant). One principal from the Caribbean elaborated,

> That important use of data, not just to overload and collect but to use it to inform any decision that takes place as it relates to the teaching and learning. It added value, really, to my understanding of data and how to use that data to create effect, to effect change. (Participant)

The use of data also had an impact on teacher efficacy, as a principal in Australia commented, "Teacher efficacy, getting a better idea of the understanding of really knowing the kids deeply and knowing data, and then moving forward that way" (Participant).

The notions of *effecting change* to student learning and "moving forward" was in the context of teachers working together and collaborating on the use of data from a whole of school perspective as one principal described, "It wasn't about the individual teacher or the teacher's role in it, it was everybody's input into that child" (Participant). As two school leaders further elaborated,

> We got into data and what it's really about with all the perspectives and all the things you observe and all the conversations you have. All the things that you know, making the whole picture. . . . They are inspired to continue to understand the power of data use. . . . our ultimate goal is to have the visible data and for me to go in to each class and see that this student has moved from there to there. (Participant)

Leading in and though data was also linked to fostering the learning organization and/or embracing collaborative learning cultures based on positive relationships of trust, as a principal in Australia outlined: "The collaborative inquiry we're on our way to doing those sorts of things, creating that culture, through the professional learning communities and, you know, the data collection" (Participant). Another school leader commented, "What we did together as a team, we looked at the broad school improvement plan, but we were able to come up with an action plan using that data to support our students" (Participant).

It was clear that for many principals leading through data further empowered the ownership of student learning by everybody, which in turn empowered decision making around quality learning from a more collaborative and targeted approach. Positive relationships built upon trust helped bring staff together to constructively use data to inform a whole-school approach to student learning, which was found to support effective change in the schools. This positive change was not only related to student achievement but to the culture and organization of the schools around quality learning and teaching at the individual student, classroom, and school level.

This section identified three universal themes that school leaders found the most important in terms of the professional learning that impacted their practice in their schools. These themes were found to be intricately interrelated in how they were applied by school leaders in the complex and multidimensional context of their schools and further demonstrated how the ISL program effectively supported school leaders to successfully deal with the realities of school leadership in modern schools across the globe.

The next section will explore what matters most for school leaders when it comes to the design and delivery principles that should inform universal school leadership programs.

WHAT MATTERS MOST: PROGRAM DESIGN AND DELIVERY

As indicated above, evidence from the three international case studies pointed to a number of universal principles for the design and delivery of professional learning for school leaders. The guiding principles that focus on program structure, content, instructional strategies, instructors, and participants are interrelated and tightly connected. Arguably, all must be applied in concert to achieve excellence.

What Matters Most in Terms of Program Structure?

Overall, the program structure should address the realities of the challenging jobs of the participants in terms of availability, amount of time required, organization of content, and assessment demands. One participant in particular captured the issue:

> [it] was good in that, whilst it was online, and it was a time commitment to do it online, you could sit down and do it, you know, a bit each night, which is like half an hour to an hour. And it didn't feel like I'd have to sit down each night for three or four hours and, you know, slog my way through it, you knew you could come home, you could just go, yeah, okay, I'm going to spend an hour now and do this, and do it comfortably, so I felt the online bit was paced well. (Participant)

Utilizing a blend of online, onsite, and hybrid delivery is an important strategy in providing this flexibility. Even with onsite delivery, an online environment can be used to manage content, establish ongoing collaboration, record reflections, and generally extend the learning: "the face-to-face modules were fantastic for that [collaboration], and maintaining that after the time has been really good"(Participant).

We further suggest that it is important to organize the program in discrete units of study, tied together by an overarching conceptual framework. This framework needs to reflect a current and inspirational image of the school leader and, most importantly, must provide participants with the fundamental building blocks for learning: "this is kind of what ISL has done for me. It's kind of given me the big picture. It has made me see the cohesion" (Participant). Relatedly, we believe a certificate structure offers the ability to bind all of the components into a thoughtful, comprehensive learning experience: "everything else I'd done was a workshop here and a workshop there" (Participant).

Time is another key consideration in program design. Evidence indicated that participants required time between units to not only reflect on and consolidate their learning, but time to apply the new learning. Consequently, in establishing the overall length of the program, the time between the learning sessions must be appropriately planned, considering both the school year calendar and demands on the leader. As one participant commented: "And that's probably one of, whether it's conscious or unconscious, [the] effects of doing the program over such a long period of time you can actually be doing it, you're experimenting on your own school" (Participant).

What Matters Most in Terms of Content?

Comments from participants also revealed the importance of providing tools that can be utilized with little or no modification by the leader. These tools, including frameworks, articles, and process models, are all designed to be used with teaching staff. For participants, these provided actionable items: "It was a functional PD, I think, for me, it was something I could come back and use straight away" (Participant).

Programs should also provide for the inclusion of local resources and priorities: "I think having that local context will help the program, so it's sort of less Canadian" (Participant). That stated, tools, research, and literature from around the world are highly valued: "[T]he readings were good. They were relevant, and they were focused on what we were doing and what we needed at the time" (Participant). Participants, in fact, make sense of specific resources in their context during discussions, reflections, and applications.

What Matters Most in Terms of Instructional Strategies?

In designing and delivering the learning experience for leaders, it is critical to demonstrate strategies that can be directly replicated by the school leader in their own school. As noted by one participant: "the practical assignments we were given and [I] probably used every one of them with my staff and colleagues" (Participant). Another participant further suggested: "It's the strategies that we are using in different topics that we could use with staff and the staff could, in the end, use it with their students."

These strategies should be based on adult learning principles, with opportunities for reading, listening, speaking, reflection, movement, collaboration, and discussion: "The way it was run, the collegiality, to be able to work in the groups and to have the conversations and work through it, it was great" (Participant).

Furthermore, participants need to be given the opportunity to discuss the strategies from the perspective of a facilitator. And finally, programs should require participants to demonstrate deep reflection on the content, process, and potential for application in the leadership role. One participant nicely summarizes:

> It was a good presentation backed by research and video clips and you know, it was interactive and fun. The pace was always kind of changing. . . . did an excellent job of that, but then that I could take away and actually have some goodies that I can try out and actually use other than just the research. (Participant)

Programs also need to provide for a culminating project that requires the participant to apply their new learning to a real leadership challenge, with the guidance of the instructor and mentor: "I think the ultimate thing that probably had the biggest impact directly on this school was the actual project that we had to develop" (Participant). "I feel like ISL gives me kind of an action plan and it's about doing things for the teachers that I would like them to do in the classroom" (Participant).

What Matters Most in Terms of Instructors?

The best participants, content, strategies, and structure matter, but what matters the most is likely the quality of the program instructor. In judging quality, evidence points to a number of indicators that should guide selection processes.

First, instructors need to have evidence of excellence in the role of school leader and be able to provide actionable feedback: "[instructors] were really, really good, and the feedback from them was always really good . . . actionable feedback . . . it's not just been words, it's been actionable" (Participant).

Second, instructors need to have extensive experience in teaching adults and understand their learning needs: "very experienced and hands-on and you didn't feel like you were being lectured to" (Participant). "[Instructors] have been really flexible . . . 'I haven't been able to do this, I'm definitely going to finish it, but I just haven't got there,' and as long as you communicate, I guess, they've been flexible" (Participant).

And, finally, instructors need to demonstrate a passion and commitment to the learning of others with evidence of long-term mentoring relationships that reach beyond the confines of the program expectations: "having a mentor that takes care of you in that way that [instructor] does. If you have any questions, that, "Oh, I'll send you an article about that." You feel it's like a neverending support that you're going to get. It's great" (Participant).

What Matters Most in Terms of Participants?

Although literature points to the establishment of homogenous cohorts based on a rigorous selection process (Hallinger et al., 2018), thereby creating professional learning connections with a common understanding of the role, research, and strategies, our research suggested that it may not be the cohort model that is critical, but rather the degree of collaboration within the local organizational culture.

For example, in Scandinavia, the delivery model did not involve the creation of a cohort. Rather, individuals joined the onsite and online modules as time permitted, with some degree of overlap among the participants; however, collaboration among participants from various districts was reported. In the Caribbean, the delivery involved cohorts, including principals, deputies, and aspiring school leaders. However, collaboration among one another was reported to a lesser degree. It may be that the culture of the district was not conducive to collaboration or that the mandatory participation influenced the level of collaboration.

In contrast, in the Australian case, collaboration among the participants was reported as a very important aspect of the program and many other examples of connections within the district were cited. The research, therefore, suggested that the cohort model of delivery does not guarantee broad collaboration nor is it required to achieve high levels of professional learning connections.

Our research also found that the nature of the impact of the program varies from one participant to another based on prior learning, prior experience, context, tenure, and opportunity to enact new or modified practices. Indeed, the impact on the practices of school leaders is now understood as a multilayer continuum that traces the level of impact against certain criteria such as role, tenure in role and/or school, school culture, and prior knowledge. Each participant, therefore, regardless of characteristics, experiences the same learning, but applies it to practice in very different ways. This finding makes a strong argument for heterogeneous groupings or a least the questioning of the homogenous arrangement.

The size of the cohort is another factor to consider. With groups of twelve to thirty, the aims of the program can be met with important bonding between participants. Perhaps more importantly, the connection between the instructor and the individual participants can be maximized, thereby setting the stage for a mentoring relationship (noted above) after the conclusion of the program.

The principle that emerges from this discussion is to create programs for and delivered to heterogeneous groupings of leaders, thereby ensuring the diversity of learners in order to elevate dissonance and the quality of discussions.

WHAT IS NEXT

The findings of our inquiry naturally led to what should happen next in terms of school leader practice and further research in quality design and delivery of universal principal professional learning. In answer, we offer the following recommendations.

Recommendation 1: Providers of programs should use the key points of learning and universal design principles to assess and modify current programs, as well as to create new ones. In this application process, it is critical to integrate these two components to ensure an educative process that models the key learnings.

In particular, school leadership programs should provide for a culminating activity that extends beyond the typical capstone project. It needs to be more than the intellectual and academic experience of applying new knowledge to a problem of practice in collaboration with the instructor and mentor. It must be a plan that is executed within their role, supported by a mentor, and aligned with school priorities, thereby providing the pinnacle of learning opportunities.

Recommendation 2: Future research should continue to focus on what matters the most in professional learning for school leaders in terms of program structure, content, strategies, instructor, and participants. Today's answers may not reflect the leadership needs in the future.

Recommendation 3: Future research should probe the issue of universal design principles for fully online leadership programs.

CONCLUSIONS

The three international case studies have provided insight into what matters most for school leaders in their professional learning and the design and implementation of this professional learning. Three key learnings found to matter most for school leaders included: (1) it is about students and everybody knowing they are learning; (2) leading in and through relationship; and (3) leading through data.

A number of universal design principles were also identified as mattering most for school leaders that will help inform current programs and the development of future professional learning for school leaders. These highlight the importance of program structure, context, instructional strategies, instructor, and participants. The integration of key learnings with the design principles in an educative process that models the key learnings was also found to be important.

REFERENCES

Asuga, G., Eacott, S., and Scevak, J. (2015). School leadership preparation and development in Kenya. *International Journal of Educational Management, 29* (3), 355–67.

Clarke, S., Wildy, H., and Styles, I. (2011). Fit for purpose? Western Australian insights into the efficacy of principal preparation. *Journal of Educational Administration, 49*(2), 166–78.

Devin, M. (2016). *Transforming the preparation of leaders into a true partnership model. Educational Considerations, 43*(4), 15–24.

Eacott, S. (2013). The return on school leadership preparation and development programmes. *International Journal of Educational Management, 27*(7), 686–99.

Easley, J., and Tulowitzki, P. (2013). Policy formation of intercultural and globally minded educational leadership preparation. *International Journal of Educational Management, 27*(7), 744–61.

Fuller, E., Young, M., and Baker, B. D. (2010). Do principal preparation programs influence student achievement through the building of teacher-team qualifications by the principal? An exploratory analysis. *Educational Administration Quarterly, 47*(1), 173–216.

Hallinger, P., Adams, D., Harris, A., and Jones, M. S. (2018). Review of conceptual models and methodologies in research on principal instructional leadership in Malaysia. *Journal of Educational Administration, 56*(1), 104–26.

McCarthy, M. (2015). Reflections on the evolution of educational leadership preparation programs in the United States and challenges ahead. *Journal of Educational Administration, 53*(3), 416–38.

Ministry of Education. (Winter 2012–2013). Five core capacities of effective leaders. Ontario Leadership Strategy, Bulletin 1. http://www.edu.gov.on.ca/eng/policyfunding/leadership/ideasintoActionBulletin1.pdf.

Ng, A. Y. M. (2017). School leadership preparation in Malaysia: Aims, content and impact. *Educational Management Administration and Leadership, 45*(6), 1002–19.

Onguko, B., Abdalla, M., and Webber, C. (2008). Mapping principal preparation in Kenya and Tanzania. *Journal of Educational Administration, 46*(6), 715–26.

Piggot-Irvine, E., and Youngs, H. (2011). Aspiring principal development programme evaluation in New Zealand. *Journal of Educational Administration, 49*(5), 513–41.

Schaefer, B. (2015, October 12). On becoming a leader: Building relationships and creating communities. *Educause Review*. https://er.educause.edu/articles/2015/10/on-becoming-a-leader-building-relationships-and-creating-communities.

Sinek, S. (2011). *Start with why: How great leaders inspire everyone to take action.* New York, NY: Penguin.

Chapter Two

Preparation of School Leaders in China

Past to Present Practices

Tak Cheung Chan, Zhiding Shu, and Dehua Liu

School leadership in the international perspective provides a great forum for discussion. There is much to learn from educational leaders from one country to another through sharing of their professional leadership experiences. International scholars and practitioners of educational leadership can understand one another's backgrounds and challenges that make their leadership operation particularly unique and exciting. Leadership preparation programs all over the world have undergone changes to meet particular needs of their countries at different times. They are employing proven successful strategies in preparing highly capable school leaders.

The purpose of writing this chapter about school leadership in China is to echo the many success stories of a global educational-leadership perspective. School-leadership preparation programs in one country can learn from programs of other countries to see how and why leadership preparation programs are developed in such unique ways to meet countries' specific needs. It is important to recognize the culture and traditions of a country in order to have a better understanding of the background of the educational settings of the country.

In this chapter, the literature of Chinese school leadership is explored through searches of current academic journals and professional documents. Following the review of literature on school leadership, the authors continue to recall the background and historical development of school-principal preparation in China. An analysis of the highlights of current representative school-leadership preparation programs in Chinese universities was conducted to examine how these educational-leadership preparation programs reflect the school leadership literature as reviewed in the chapter.

CURRENT ISSUES ON CHINESE SCHOOL LEADERSHIP

Barney and Zhang (2009) claimed that both the empirical and nonempirical literature identified on school leadership in China relied heavily on imported Western leadership models. However, as a result of an in-depth search on current literature on the current issues of Chinese principalship, the authors found that some items of literature on Chinese school leadership can be classified as types of school leadership: leadership styles, instructional leadership, and leadership strategies. These significant pieces of school leadership literature are embedded in government documents, books, newsletters, and journal articles published in China.

TYPES OF SCHOOL LEADERSHIP

Wang and Ren (2012) identified three types of principal leadership: the "performance-oriented" principals, "performance- and research-oriented" principals, and the "expert-type" principals. "Performance-oriented" principals focus their work on basic learning of knowledge and skills needed to perform their daily duties. Additionally, "Performance- and research-oriented" principals are also interested to know why some leadership strategies work better than others. "Expert-type" principals can apply what they learn about leadership knowledge and skills to practical situations and serve as mentors to inspire others to be successful school principals.

Leadership Style

Authoritative Leadership

Zhang (1998) claimed that even though Chinese school principals wanted to maintain substantial authority over certain areas of school administration, they were leaning toward a more democratic leadership style. Contrarily, Lo (2004) stated that school principals in China were highly respected figures and their supreme authority over all school business has been known. Kao (2005) agreed with Lo that school leaders in China were simply government voice makers. Furthermore, the Professional Standards of Principals (Ministry of Education, 2013) also upheld the principals' authorities in fulfilling their daily responsibilities.

Moral Leadership

In China, school principals are held to a high level of moral leadership (Liu, 2008). Li (2011) also claimed that as an educational leader of a school in a local community, a school principal is highly respected and should be held accountable to role modeling high ethical standards. Tao (2011) further developed areas to uphold principals' moral standards to include setting up moral values, role modeling, and promoting moral values in school.

Shared Leadership

Zhang (2010) believed that school principals needed to maintain a shared leadership with his/her faculty, staff, and community to be successful. Zhang (2010) collected data through personal interviews and observations with teachers, staff, and parents of local schools. She found that school principals need to learn to support teachers and staff to share their responsibilities. She also emphasized that school principals need to stay connected with parents to solicit their opinions about the education of their children. Shared leadership is meant to build personal relationship with teachers, staff, and school communities.

Instructional Leadership

School principals as curriculum leaders ensure successful implementation of curriculum (Shi, 2008). They need to learn to implement and evaluate curriculum and facilitate its supporting resources (Xia, 2012; Zhou and Xia, 2009). Luo and Xue (2010) concluded that principal preparation programs need to include curriculum leadership as a significant component. Zheng (2012) also noted that in matters of curriculum and instruction, principals should be capable of setting instructional goals, developing instructional activities, seeking resources, and establishing procedures of instruction evaluation.

Zhao and Liu (2010) worked on developing a Chinese instructional-leadership model by employing interviewing and surveying methodology. Their entire curriculum-leadership model showed that principals' curriculum leadership in Chinese schools consisted of four dimensions: leading instructional organizations, designing instructional activities, creating instructional conditions, and supervising teaching. To ensure successful implementation of school curriculum, Chu and Liu (2010) further recommended that principals should make a routine schedule to connect frequently with teachers and observe classes on a regular basis.

Leadership Strategies

In studying practical strategies employed by school principals in their daily school operation, Li, Li, and Lu (2012) found some leadership strategies commonly agreed by principals to be effectively employed in their schools. These include inviting guest specialists to conduct workshops for teachers, supporting teachers by offering assistance after class observation, and encouraging teachers to conduct action research in their classes to verify teaching and learning outcomes.

Principals participating in the study by Jiang, Chen, and Lu (2010) were professionally polite for not identifying their own strategies that contribute to school success. Instead, they mentioned other contributing factors such as professional capacity of teachers, policy and resource support from local education entities, and the qualifications of the students enrolled in school. For sure, school leadership strategies have worked from behind the scenes to strongly support these determinant factors for school success.

BACKGROUND OF SCHOOL LEADER PREPARATION IN CHINA

The roles of school principals have been considered by Chinese policy makers to be crucial to the success of schools. A school principal has always been considered as a role model, not only for teachers and students in school but also for the entire community. In the 1950s, the Central Institute of Educational Administration was established under the Ministry of Education specifically for school principal preparation. The institute set an example for many local institutes to follow suit.

Local institutes of teacher preparation were encouraged to join the central government's effort in principal preparation with focus on the ideological and political aspects of leadership. Then, principal preparation programs in these institutes served more of a political purpose than for the learning of leadership knowledge and skills. The main curriculum offered by the institutes included philosophy, pedagogy, and psychology (Chu and Cravens, 2010). Then, in the mid-1960s, principal preparation programs were stopped for almost two decades because of the Cultural Revolution. All the principal preparation programs of the institutions were closed down.

However, since the late 1970s, educational development in China has undergone tremendous changes along with China's national open policies in international connections. What is taught in school has to support the rapid economic development of the country. In 1982, the State Education Council issued a document to clarify the preparation of elementary and secondary school principals in China. The document included the statement of philosophy, purposes, requirements, content, and means of principal preparation (Wu, Feng, and Zhou, 2000). Local education institutes were asked to participate in developing the principal preparation program.

After a few years of implementation, it was found that principals, after going through such program preparation, still could not meet the increasingly demanding requirements of principals' work (State Education Council, 1989). Thus, the State Education Council issued another document in 1989, *On Strengthening the Training for Principals of Elementary and Secondary Schools Nation-wide* (State Education Council, 1989), to focus the principal preparation programs on new professional qualifications and requirements.

The State Education Council specified for the first time in China that school principals needed to participate in the preparation program to be certified. To tighten up the activities of the principal preparation program, the State Education Council developed additional perspectives in 1995 to include three principals' preparation levels, to encourage localization of programs, and to invite university participation in the principal preparation program. However, this new initiative was not effectively implemented due to shortage of trainers, insufficient incentives, and lack of skill training (Feng, 2005).

In December 1999, a comprehensive *Guidelines for Preparation of Elementary and Secondary School Principals* was released by the Ministry of Education to cover significant areas of principal preparation nationwide (Ministry of Education, 1999). Guidelines were established for the contents, formats, organization, administration, and accountabilities of the principal preparation programs. The document mandated the basic requirements of principal certification and participation in continuous advanced-preparation programs.

As stated in the document, foundations of school principal preparation were established: the National Institute of Educational Administration by the central government, the Center for Preparation of Elementary School Principals in Beijing Normal University, and the Center for Preparation of Secondary School Principals in East China Normal University. To respond to the central government's effort of school principal preparation, provinces, cities, and districts also established principal preparation centers of different levels.

Then, the *Outline of Basic Education Curriculum Reform* (Ministry of Education, 2001) was issued to aim for a student-centered policy with innovative educational approaches to include creativity, collaboration, engagement, problem-solving skills, and knowledge applications. School principals were expected to play a major role in implementing the curriculum reform guidelines as outlined by the central government. Additionally, school leaders were encouraged to generate supplementary academic activities to the curriculum guidelines to suit the needs of their schools.

In the years following, the delivery of the Basic Education Curriculum Reform was not without difficulty. Many school principals had not received sufficient preparation to perform all the functions as curriculum leaders (Su, Adams, and Mininberg, 2000). They were accused of poor leadership in curriculum development and implementation (Luo and Xue, 2010). A more stringent system of educational supervision and accountability was needed to ensure efficient and effective implementation of the educational reform.

As a result, the *Professional Standards of Principals at the Compulsory Education Stage* was released in 2013 (Ministry of Education, 2013). These standards specified the roles and responsibilities of school principals in the effective delivery of school leadership. Principals were recognized as instructional leaders and given increased responsibilities of curriculum supervision and evaluation in addition to other miscellaneous work for school operation.

THE CONTENTS OF GOVERNMENT PROGRAMS FOR SCHOOL PRINCIPAL PREPARATION

The traditional competencies of principals in modern Chinese schools have been explicitly accounted for in Chinese education literature for years. In the early 1950s, most school principals did not receive much of a formal preparation to be educational leaders. In fact, many school principals were promoted to the principalship because of their outstanding performance in their previous teaching positions. Many school principals were receiving on-the-job training and learning to be a school principal by trial and error. They were not aware of the competencies they needed to possess while serving as school principals (Jiang 1986).

School principals' full scope of daily duties was clearly stated in the *On Strengthening the Training for Principals of Elementary and Secondary Schools Nation-wide*, a document issued by the State Education Council in 1989. Goals were established by the State Education Council to prepare school principals, who were expected to possess the following competencies after program preparation:

- Ability to develop plans for the school;
- Ability to implement ideological, political, and moral education;
- Ability to facilitate student overall growth;
- Ability to conduct school instructional activities;
- Ability to support teacher professional development;
- Ability to lead groups;
- Ability to coordinate with parents and school communities;
- Ability to meet new challenges;
- Ability to analyze results of instructional innovations for student learning improvement; and
- Ability to present oral and written reports professionally.

The areas of preparation in school principal competencies in China were also noted by Jiang and Chan (1990), who asserted that school principals needed to be prepared to work with school organization, school law, educational planning, personnel management, school financial operation, curriculum development, instructional supervision, educational evaluation, resource management, and school–community relations. Additionally, school principals should be prepared with skills to resolve any new issues and meet challenges in the daily operation of their school.

The most comprehensive coverage of content for school-principal preparation programs in China were specified by the *Guidelines for Preparation of Elementary and Secondary School Principals* (Ministry of Education, 1999). The guidelines pinpointed the following areas that all school-principal preparation programs need to incorporate: theories of politics, ethical considerations, educational policies and law, theories and practices of modern education, theories and practices of school administration, modern educational technology, modern scientific knowledge, and human sociology.

CHARACTERISTICS OF GOVERNMENT EFFORT IN SCHOOL LEADERSHIP PREPARATION

After the Cultural Revolution, the four areas of national modernization came to include industry, agriculture, national defense, and scientific technology. However, the backbone of the modernization movement is the development of education in which school principals play the leading role. Therefore, China has placed the preparation of school leaders as a crucial priority. In the past forty years, the central government has issued significant announcements to establish, improve, and renew the principal preparation program with the purpose of creating the most efficient and effective principals to meet new challenges.

These tireless efforts in developing school-leadership preparation programs are characterized by six features. First, the central government has always been in the forefront of principal leadership preparation. A four-level system of principal preparation (central government, province, city, and district) has started to promote many opportunities for principals to participate in professional preparation activities.

Second, the determination of the central government to prepare high-quality school principalship is unquestionable. It started in 1982 in the call for establishing the principal preparation program nationwide, and a document by the State Education Council in 1989 helped strengthen the implementation of the preparation programs. The loopholes of the 1982 and 1989 documents were then tightened up by a 1995 State Education Council announcement. Subsequently, the 1999 guidelines for principal preparation were followed by the professional standards of principal preparation in 2013.

Third, it was established in the 1999 guidelines that a system of continuous improvement of school principal preparation would serve as an encouragement for professional advancement. All basic principal certificates need to be renewed every five years. They are replaced with an advanced principal certificate after participation in higher level leadership preparation. A professional point system is also established to provide additional incentives for participation in advanced-level programs.

Fourth, the contents of the principal preparation programs have continued to be broadened from simply concentrating on political ideologies to all areas of school administration. The contents of recent preparation programs have displayed the inclusion of technological leadership as an essential component of the programs.

Fifth, the most recent programs have demonstrated a new approach to school principal preparation. In addition to learning as a basic component, the programs also invite participating principals to explore the background and social and cultural environments in which administrative strategies are implemented. Some senior principals also serve as mentors for novice principals.

Sixth, as a result of social competition, principals have been pressured by parents and local communities to improve student achievement. This is reflected in the trend of development in principal preparation programs. More and more emphasis has been given to preparing school principals to be instructional leaders so that they can serve as teacher supervisors, instructional program developers, and program evaluators.

PRINCIPAL PREPARATION PROGRAM IN INSTITUTES OF HIGHER EDUCATION

The authors have identified prestigious Chinese school-leadership preparation programs in higher education for follow-up studies. Selection of school-leadership preparation programs was based on the recommendations of Chinese scholars with focus on unique program qualities. Geographical locations of the leadership preparation programs were also considered in selection to keep a representative balance. Program development handbooks and detailed information about program implementation were studied with in-depth elaboration of programs from responsible faculty members of the programs.

Since the 1995 announcement by the State Education Council, universities have been invited to participate in developing and implementing programs of school principal preparation. Some universities started with offering certification programs of principal preparation while some have developed graduate-school programs at the master's and doctorate levels. Four universities offering principal preparation programs have been selected for reporting in this chapter.

The first university is in North China, and is known for its leadership in academic partnerships with other Chinese and overseas universities. It has served the local elementary and secondary schools with their unique programs of preparing educators. The university offers graduate programs in economics and administration of education. Courses emphasize school administration, international political and economic development, economics and administration of educational systems, and management of school and society relationship. The university works with local school systems in conducting school leadership research projects.

The second university, also located in North China, offers a doctoral program in educational administration and innovation. With support from the central government, the program contains three emphases: education administration and policy, school leadership and management, and human resource management in education. The program has an international feature striving to advance the frontier of human knowledge in the field of educational administration and to facilitate education change worldwide.

The curriculum includes courses in Chinese culture, policies and management, research methods, literature on educational leadership, human resource management, educational policy studies, education planning, international education, and educational leadership practicum. Additionally, the university also offers a master's degree in comparative educational leadership and policy. The program is designed to prepare individuals for globalization in the fields of educational management, leadership, and policy making worldwide. The program is usually offered in collaboration with school leadership programs of other countries.

Located in Central China, the third university has a service-orientation goal. With special support from the city government, the university offers school leadership workshops, seminars, and certification programs to prepare school leaders. The Educational Leadership Center was established to plan and organize school leader preparatory activities. The center also publishes professional journals and hosts professional conferences. With its broad connections with many universities worldwide, the center stands in the forefront of international educational strategies. However, the center does not offer any academic degree programs in educational leadership.

The fourth university is in South China and offers a doctoral program, a master's program, and certification programs of leadership to suit particular students' needs. The doctoral program is designed for experienced educators and professionals in education settings who aspire to extend their expertise in a particular area of educational administration. Many hours of the program are involved with research projects. The master's program is focused on developing leaders with the capacity to operate successfully in an international leadership environment and lead educational changes.

The certification programs include the general certification of leadership practices and the advanced certification of leadership research. They are designed for educators and administrators who want to improve their leadership capabilities or career aspirations. The programs include school-based research projects and deep reflection on personal leadership practices.

In view of the educational leadership programs in these four representative universities in China, the authors have made the following observations:

1. The universities have established school-leader preparation programs with their specific goals to achieve. Some research-oriented universities have developed programs with heavy emphasis on school-based research projects. Some universities have preferred to work collaboratively with local schools and districts in developing more practice-oriented activities for the improvement of leadership skills.
2. All four universities have made strong national and international connections by faculty exchanges and program collaboration. Some universities even offer the program delivery in the English language to facilitate participation of international students.
3. All four universities have school leadership programs with courses covering the most updated content and with high technology use. Some universities have even developed over half of their course offerings online.
4. Since school leadership is strongly associated with human relationships, all the school leadership programs have advertised to provide networking opportunities and practicum experiences to enrich individuals' learning processes.
5. These four representative universities are publicly funded either by the central government or by local city governments. Therefore, these universities are able to develop very effective leadership programs to meet the needs of the community. They are able to attract top-quality students to strengthen the student body and recruit academically authoritative professors in support of their programs. On the other hand, these public universities are also held accountable for the quality of their graduates' performance.

CONNECTION BETWEEN EDUCATIONAL LEADERSHIP LITERATURE AND PRACTICES

At one time in the development of Chinese educational leadership, scholars could not locate an educational leadership model that China could claim its own (Barney and Zhang, 2009). However, the review of literature in this chapter has identified four categories of educational leadership models in China: types of educational leadership, leadership style, instructional leadership, and leadership strategies. Many Chinese educational-leadership practices in recent years are connected to these educational leadership models.

Types of Principal Leadership

The 1995 State Education Council document required that school principals need to be certified with basic leadership knowledge and skills. The 1999 *Guidelines for Preparation of Elementary and Secondary School Principals* clearly specified the levels of principal preparation as (1) preparation for minimum requirements; (2) preparation of advanced veteran principals; and (3) preparation of senior principals. Wang and Ren (2012) referred to these classifications as "performance-oriented" principals, "performance- and research-oriented" principals, and "expert-type" principals. University programs have also specified programs to be practitioner oriented or research based.

Leadership Styles

Lo (2004) and Kao (2005) agreed that school principals in China assumed their authoritative position as heads of schools and executors of government educational policies. Their observations are reflected in the 1999 *Guidelines for Preparation of Elementary and Secondary School Principals* by which the central government took the lead in establishing principal preparation institutes. Many provinces, cities, and districts also followed by setting up institutes for principal preparation. In addition, the *Professional Standards of Principals* (Ministry of Education 2013) further empowered school principals in their daily duties.

The moral aspects of *Professional Standards of Principals* (Ministry of Education 2013) also set stringent rules regarding the personal and professional behavior of school principals to be followed. This echoed what Liu (2008) and Li (2011) noted in that school principals in Chinese communities are held to high ethical standards.

Zhang (2010) believed that school principals could perform their duties with a shared leadership style by which they stay connected with their school teachers, staff, and local communities. This shared leadership style has been exercised by the central government by inviting local governments and universities to participate in the preparation of school principals. The 1999 *Guidelines for Preparation of Elementary and Secondary School Principals* have also strongly encouraged senior school principals to share their professional experiences with beginning school principals to help with their professional development.

Instructional Leadership

Zhao and Liu's (2010) instructional leadership model consisted of four components: leading instructional organizations, designing instructional activities, creating instructional conditions, and supervising teaching. To address the need for instructional leadership training, the Shanghai Municipal Education Commission (2010) initiated the *Three-Year Action Plan to Promote Curriculum Leadership of Secondary and Primary School (and Kindergarten) Principals* to develop principals' knowledge and skills in curriculum leadership.

However, the central government's effort in establishing school principal's instructional leadership role could be recalled in the *Outline of Basic Education Curriculum Reform* (Ministry of Education, 2001). In 2013, the *Professional Standards of Principals at the Compulsory Education Stage* further added curriculum supervision and evaluation as major responsibilities of school principals.

At the university level, an examination of the school-principal preparation programs in China indicated that curriculum development and instructional leadership play a major role in all the content areas of the programs. An important goal of the leadership preparation program is that graduates will work comfortably with teachers, parents, and community members in the development, implementation, and evaluation of school curriculum for the best learning benefits of the students.

Leadership Strategies

Li, Li, and Lu (2012) found that the most common leadership strategies school principals used were related closely to supporting teachers. These strategies included providing teachers with professional development and supporting teaching responsibilities. Back in 1989, the State Education Council had already established goals to prepare school principals. Principals were expected to meet the goals by possessing abilities to employ leadership strategies in their administrative work to include strategies in conducting instructional activities, supporting teacher professional development, and analyzing the results of instructional innovations.

IMPLICATIONS FOR EDUCATIONAL PLANNING

The analysis of literature and practices in school leadership of China as outlined in this chapter has significant implications for the planning of educational leadership programs and the practice of school leadership. Even though the analysis was made with reference to China, the significance of the analysis can be applied to any educational leadership situation worldwide. International educators can learn from one another by sharing their unique experiences.

Planning for Leadership Preparation

In planning for educational leadership development programs, a strong message has to be delivered to all aspiring school leaders that successful school leaders play many roles and undertake multiple responsibilities. The eventual goal is to achieve student success. Perhaps consideration has to be given to initiating a strong school-administrative internship program to demonstrate a good balance of a school leader's daily work. School-leadership preparation programs in China have set an excellent example of international connection and also have varied their instructional approaches to facilitate a wide variety of student backgrounds.

Planning for School Leadership Practices

The results of this analysis indicate the need for a school principal to possess multiple administrative skills. A school principal has to follow government educational guidelines in the delivery of his/her responsibilities. All the school activities under his/her leadership need to be student-centered for the development of the whole child. Additionally, a successful school is one that displays collaborative effort between all stakeholders in the relationship-building process. Among all the contributing factors to school success, school leaders play the key leadership role through goal setting and implementation.

CONCLUSION

It is obvious that increased international competitiveness has made the work of school leaders more difficult through pressure to enhance student success. School-leadership preparation programs of different countries have much to share in their unique experiences in preparing school leaders. The Chinese experiences of school leadership preparation can contribute much to the international setting.

Through the academic analysis in this chapter, readers have a better understanding of how Chinese school-leader preparation programs are developed through a professional path. They are highlighted by government leadership with local and university participation, broadening the horizon in program development, inclusion of innovative delivery approaches, and involvement of international perspectives. The development of school-principal preparation programs in China is solid and is taking a step-by-step approach to meeting the challenges of the country's needs.

REFERENCES

Barney, J. B., and Zhang, S. J. (2009). The future of Chinese management research: A theory of Chinese management versus a Chinese theory of management. *Management and Organization Review, 5*, 15–28.

Chu, H., and Craven, X. C. (2010). *Developing principals in China: Challenges, opportunities, and strategic development.* Paper presented at the Asian Leadership Roundtable hosted by Asia Pacific Centre for Leadership and Change, Hong Kong Institute of Education, Hong Kong.

Chu, H. Q., and Liu, J. (2010). Xiaozhang jiaoxue lingdaoli de tisheng [The improvement of principal instructional leadership—Commentary on whether "big principals" need to go to "small classrooms"]. *Zhongxiaoxue Guanli [Primary and Secondary School Management], 3,* 4–6.

Feng, D. (2005). Principal training and development in the People's Republic of China: Retrospect and prospect. In P. Hallinger (Ed.), *Reshaping the landscape of school leadership development: A global perspective* (pp. 205–16). New York, NY: Taylor & Francis.

Jiang, M. L., Chen, J. J., and Lu, P. (2010). Xuexiao neihan fazhan zhong de xiaozhang lingdaoli [Principal leadership in school improvement—A survey of 331 principals of Pudong District of Shanghai]. *Quanqiu Jiaoyu Zhanwang [Global Education], 39*(8), 78–83.

Jiang, Y. S. (1986). *The study of school administration.* Guangdong, China: Guangdong Higher Education Press.

Jiang, Y. S., and Chan, T. C. (1990). *A conceptual framework of modern educational administration.* Guangdong, China: Guangdong Higher Education Press.

Kao, T. C. (2005). *High school principals' values and their symbolic and cultural leadership approaches to character education in China* [Unpublished doctoral dissertation]. University of San Diego, San Diego, CA.

Li, X. L., Li, W. H., and Lu, N. G. (2012). Cujin jiaoshi fazhan de xiaozhang lingdaoli yanjiu. [Research on the principals' leadership for promoting teacher development: The case study of two schools' principals]. *Jiaoshi Fazhan Yanjiu [Educational Development], 4,* 70–74.

Li, Z. T. (2011). Xiaozhang ruhe shixian jiazhi lingdaoli? [How can principals enact value leadership?]. *Zhongxiaoxue Guanli [Primary and Secondary School Management], 1,* 5–7.

Liu, J. (2008). Lun xiaozhang meide [On the virtues of principals]. *Jiaoyu Lilun yu Shijian [Theory and Practice of Education], 28,* 50–53.

Lo, K. P. (2004). Adaptation and development of schooling in changing societies. In R. Koo, C. K. Kam, and M. S. Yung (Eds.), *Education and curriculum reform adaptation and development in the Pearl River Delta.* Hong Kong, China: The Association for Childhood Educational International.

Luo, Y. J., and Xue, T. Y. (2010). Kegai haiyao zai guo jidaokan [How many obstacles will curriculum reform meet]. *Shanghai Jiaoyu [Shanghai Education], 5,* 18–20.

Ministry of Education. (1999). *Guidelines for the preparation of elementary and secondary school principals.* Beijing, China.

Ministry of Education. (2001). *The curriculum reform guidelines for the nine-year compulsory education.* http://edu.cn/20010926/3002911.shtml [*Jiu Nian Mein Fei Jiao Yu De Ke Cheng Qui Hua*].

Ministry of Education. (2013). *The professional standards of principals of the compulsory education stage.* http://www.moe.edu.cn/publicfiles/business/htmlfiles/moe/s7148/201302 147899.html [*Mein Fei Jiao Yu Xue Xiao Xiao Zhang De Zhuan Ye Biao Zhun*].

Shanghai Municipal Education Commission. (2010). *On the notice of "A three-year action plan to promote curriculum leadership of secondary and primary school (and kindergarten) principals."* http://www.shmec.gov.cn/html/xxgh/201004/3022010002.php.

Shi, X. X. (2008). Tigao xiaozhang kecheng lingdaoli de sikao [Thoughts on improving principal curriculum leadership]. *Liaoning Jiaoyu Yanjiu* [*Liaoning Educational Research*], *4*, 49–50.
State Education Council. (1989). *On strengthening the training for principals of elementary and secondary schools nation-wide.* Beijing, China.
Su, Z., Adams, J., and Mininberg, E. (2000). Profiles and preparation of urban school principals: A comparative study in the United States and China. *Education and Urban Society, 32*(4), 455–80.
Tao, X. P. (2011). Tisheng xiaozhang jiazhi lingdaoli de jige zhongyao huanjie [Some key factors of improving principal value leadership]. *Zhongxiaoxue Guanli* [*Primary and Secondary School Management*], *1*, 4.
Wang, R. P., and Ren, L. H. (2012). Shilun xiaozhang chengzhang de leixing ji fazhan mubiao de zhiding [Different types of principal growth and formulation of development goals]. *Jiaoyu Daokan* [*Journal of Educational Development*], *5*, 48–49.
Wu, Z., Feng, D., and Zhou, J. (Eds.) (2000). *Educational administration: A new framework.* Shanghai, China: East China Normal University Press.
Xia, X. J. (2012). Xiaozhang kecheng lingdaoli: Xuexiao tese fazhan de yingran xuanze [Principal curriculum leadership: The default choice for developing school uniqueness]. *Jiaoyu Lilun yu Shijian* [*Theory and Practice of Education*], *32*(5), 15–18.
Zhang, S. (2010). Xiaozhang lingdaoli de tisheng [The enhancement of principal leadership]. *Jiaoyu Lilun yu Shijian* [*Theory and Practice of Education*], *7*, 22–23.
Zhang, X. (1998). *Chinese perspectives on Western concepts of educational leadership in Xi'an, China in the era of Den Xiaoping* [Unpublished doctoral dissertation]. Brigham Young University, Provo, UT.
Zhao, Q., and Liu, J. (2010). Woguo xiaozhang jiaoxue lingdaoli moxing yanjiu [Models of instructional leadership of Chinese principals]. *Zhongxiaoxue Guanli* [*Primary and Secondary School Management*], *3*, 10–13.
Zheng, J. Z. (2012). Xiaozhang jiaoxue lingdaoli chutan [A tentative study of leading force of principals]. *Hebei Shifan Daxue Xuebao* [*Journal of Hebei Normal University/Educational Science Edition*], *14*(11), 42–45.
Zhou, L. Z., and Xia, Y. J. (2009). Shilun zhongxiaoxue xiaozhang de kecheng lingdaoli [On the curriculum leadership and primary and secondary school principals]. *Shanghai Jiaoyu Keyan* [*Shanghai Educational Research*], *3*, 66–67.

Chapter Three

Complex Adaptive Leadership for School Principals (CAL-SP)

Theory and Practice in the Case of Turkish Schools

Hamit Özen and Selahattin Turan

Up to the mid-twentieth century, most scientific disciplines accepted the phenomena of deterministic, which is using or believing in the idea that everything is caused by another event or action and so you are not free to choose what you do. This deterministic approach required dividing the whole into pieces to understand it better. Organizations, knowledge, the nature of humans, and also leadership were thought of as deterministic and they were reduced to pieces, neglecting the complex nature of the phenomena (Obolensky, 2010).

The principle of reduction inevitably results in the simplification of the complex phenomena, which might obscure the truth and eliminate all elements that cannot be measured and quantified; taking the human out of what is human—the passions, emotions, sorrows, and joys. Furthermore, when the principle of reduction is applied in strict obedience to the determinist postulate, it obscures what is fortuitous, new, and inventive (Morin, 1999).

However, a rapid change in technology, economics, and the social, political, and cultural aspects of a complex world has forced reform in educational systems in several countries. This set of changes proposes a growing awareness of the requisite to develop preparation of students for productive functioning in the highly demanding environment. Thus, it is necessary to consider the complexity of the education system itself and the multitude of problems that must be addressed (Patton, 2011).

Actually, no simple, single approach can be employed with a hope that significant improvements to the system will occur. However, new theories have been emerging to understand the organizations better (Koopmans, 2015). More specifically, complexity theory (CT) is an interdisciplinary theory that examines uncertainty and nonlinearity in open systems such as education systems and schools.

CT emphasizes interactions and the accompanying feedback loops that constantly change systems. It proposes that while systems are unpredictable, they are also constrained by order-generating rules bringing new ideals for leadership (Burnes, 2005). Furthermore, complex adaptive leadership for school principals (CAL-SP), which is a complementary approach to leadership based on a polyarchic assumption (i.e., leadership of the many by the many), rather than based on an oligarchic assumption (i.e., leadership of the many by the few) (Ford, 2010), is premised on several critical notions that will be explained below.

First, CAL-SP has the ability to establish informal dynamics embedded in the school context referring to the nature of interactions among school partners (Uhl-Bien, Marion, and McKelvey, 2007). Second, CAL-SP distinguishes leadership and leaders. Leadership is accepted as emergent and comprised of interactive dynamics that produce outcomes at the school by all school partners (Heifetz, 1994; Uhl-Bien et al., 2007). The CAL-SP model intends to eradicate the notion of the leader as a periphery, which disregards the essential nature of leadership as a process.

Third, CAL-SP helps to distinguish school leadership from managerial positions or from principal posts (Uhl-Bien et al., 2007). The majority of school leadership research has investigated leadership in formal and managerial roles (Bedeian and Hunt, 2006) and has not adequately addressed leadership that occurs throughout the organization embedded in the school context. This study used managerial leadership and adaptive leadership to refer to the administrative functions of school principals, such as coordinating, planning, and structuring school activities to accomplish the CAL-SP without oversimplifying it to the administrative role.

School leadership has been accepted as an important factor for effective schools and provides a catalyst for "shaking up the school house" (Schlechty, 2001) and educational systems (Fullan, 1992; Johnson, 1996). That is why in the present article, a model of CAL-SP based on the study of complexity science (Uhl-Bien et al., 2007) has been developed. CAL-SP is a modern leadership model for school principals, the propositions of which are expected to fit the dynamics of social, managerial, and organizational behavior in schools.

THEORETICAL FRAMEWORK

CAL-SP is a framework for school leadership that enables the learning, creative, and adaptive capacity of school partners in schools. This framework aims to foster complex dynamics in the school context, intending to reshape school communications interactions and bureaucracy, centralism and decentralism, enabling and coordinating, exploration and exploitation, CAS and hierarchy, and informal emergence and top-down control (Uhl-Bien et al., 2007).

CAL-SP suggests that the role of school principals not be limited to attenuate the teachers and students' skills and abilities to perform with centralized organizational aims. Rather, school principals, who are responsible for knowledge production, should act to enable informal emergence and to coordinate the school contexts to enhance the quality of education (Uhl-Bien et al., 2007).

The complex adaptive leadership (CAL) model was employed by taking into account theory-based study that was effective in uncovering managerial issues touching upon: (1) managerial leadership, including resource management, risk management, decision making (Chaffe 1983), planning, and controlling; (2) adaptive leadership, including network dynamics, change-innovation, and crisis management; and the last dimension, (3) enabling leadership, including interaction, interdependency, and ethical values (Ozen, 2015).

Managerial Leadership (ML)

Managerial leadership (ML) explains the actions of people in their managerial roles who plan, control, and coordinate organizational activities. Managerial leaders organize tasks, take part in planning, build vision and mission, need resources to reach an organization's goals (Dougherty and Hardy, 1996), manage crises and risks (Mumford et al., 2002), and make decisions (Jehn, 1997).

ML, as described by CAL, takes for granted exercising one's authority and skills with consideration of the organization's need for creativity, learning, and adaptability. ML also realizes that managers' actions can seriously impact resource management, risk management, and decision making (Chaffe, 1983), as well as planning and controlling (Uhl-Bien et al., 2007). In formal terms, resource management (RM) is defined as a component of management that takes care of the human, financial, and distribution demands of vital resources at schools.

Generally, everyone, but specifically principals, must become responsible, self-regulating, and risk-averse, attending to their own needs, and making their own provisions for the future if they can. Current risk management includes strategic, policy, market, reputational, operational, financial, asset, technological, security, workforce, regulatory, and governance risks (Leithwood, 2001).

Educational leadership and decision making are conducted in conjunction with a school's mission and values. This is the crux of CAL (Uhl-bien et al., 2007). From a rational perspective, decision making involves choice, process, and change. Controlling is another function of ML. Managers' first task is to set the strategies, make the plans and carry them out. If conditions warrant, plans are modified. This is the critical control function of management. And since management involves directing the activities of others, a major part of the control function is making sure other people do what should be done.

Adaptive Leadership (AL)

Leaders have many competing phenomena in their environment; leadership is more complex and difficult than it was in the past. Schools today are open to all kind of attractors, and are complex organizations whose internal and external elements need to be considered (Jones and Paterson, 1992). Adaptive leaders do not just make changes; they carefully recognize potential changes in the external environment and consider the best path that will positively affect the organization.

AL involves changing behavior in appropriate ways as the situation changes (Yukl and Mahsud, 2010). AL allows leaders to mobilize people to tackle tough challenges and thrive. That is why AL challenges the beliefs, values, and norms in complex dynamics, which may lead individuals to resist the ideas and changes that emerge from an AL approach (Yukl, 2010).

CAL describes the conditions in which adaptive dynamics emerge and generate creative and adaptive knowledge. This knowledge exhibits sufficient significance and impact to create change, which lets leaders emerge naturally within the context. As adaptive leaders, school principals do not act as individuals, but rather as dynamic facilitators of interdependent agents in the complex adaptive system (CAS) such as school. To exhibit significance and impact, adaptive leadership must be embedded in an appropriately structured, neural-like network of CAS and agents; it exhibits significance and impact that generates change in the social system.

AL has three dimensions. The first one is *network dynamics*. Network dynamics explain the contexts that motivate adaptive leadership. The second facet is *change and innovation*. Innovation and change are seen as applying the development of new service offerings, business models, pricing plans, and routes to market, as well as new management practices (Birkinshaw, Bouquet, and Barsoux, 2011). The last facet is *crisis management*. Crisis is seen as a risk characterized by an "event, revelation, allegation, or set of circumstances that threatens the integrity, reputation, or survival of an individual or an institution (Jones and Paterson, 1992).

Enabling Leadership (EL)

The role of enabling leadership in the CAL model is to prepare contexts that catalyze adaptive leadership and allow for the emergence of CAL. Enabling leadership (EL) is necessary for all level leaders. The functions of EL are to facilitate effective CAS dynamics by fostering conditions that catalyze and allow for the emergence of AL.

EL also includes managing the entanglement between ML and AL and organizational conditions in which AL exists. Furthermore, this process includes helping to disseminate innovative products of AL upward and through to the formal managerial system (Uhl-Bien et al., 2007). EL's purpose is to catalyze CAL, which depends on interactive relationships in interdependent contexts (Uhl-Bien et al., 2007) and ethical leadership behaviors (Ozen, 2015).

The first facet of enabling leadership is interaction to create effective networks in organizations. Interaction offers opportunities to develop a network where information channels are open. Enabling leaders do not necessarily create the sophisticated linkages; rather, their complex networks evolve and adapt to the changing context.

The second facet is interdependency. Interaction is not sufficient for CAL to emerge in context. The dynamics that bear CAL are derived from emergent conflicting constraints to readjust the system. It is a kind of win-win policy of which outcomes occur when each side of a dispute feels they have won. Since both sides benefit from such phenomena, any resolutions to the conflict are likely to be accepted voluntarily by each side.

The third facet is the ethical values of CAL. Ethics are related to leadership and value creative consciousness in organizational life. When considering ethics, definitions of leadership are focused how leaders behave in a good way. Schools as social organizations are strictly based on values and moral acts, which are placed at the center of leadership relations.

PURPOSE OF THE STUDY

The purpose of this study was to determine the degree to which school principals in Turkey practice CAL-SP in their schools as measured by the Complex Adaptive School Leadership Scale (Ozen, 2015). The following research questions guided this investigation:

1. To what degree do Turkish schoolteachers perceive their principals to be practicing CAL-SP in their schools?

2. As perceived by teachers, do perceptions of leadership practices differ based on teachers' variables, specifically gender, years of work experience, age, and union membership?

SIGNIFICANCE

Currently, there is increasing pressure being placed upon schools in Turkey to enact transformation. The pursuit of school reform and reshaping the educational system has focused on the importance of school and school leadership effectiveness. CAL-SP, which is based on the conceptual framework of Uhl-Bien and colleagues (2007) and studied by Ozen (2015), provided school principals with practical guidance on how to lead as well as practical suggestions on how to act in the complex school environment.

The results of this research served as a basis for school principals to assess their leadership strengths and weaknesses to become more effective school leaders. Furthermore, it is hoped that this research will be seen as a starting point for research in CAL-SP in Turkish schools, thereby stimulating further research to provide valuable insight for both academicians and practitioners. Until now, there has been no reported study identifying the degree to which school principals in Turkey practice CAL-SP.

DESIGN

This study is quantitative in nature and was conducted using a survey methodology. The survey was cross-sectional; the data were collected at a single point in time. A variety of statistical techniques were utilized in this research: means, standard deviations, t-tests, and one-way analysis of variance (ANOVA). Means and standard deviations were used to measure the degree to which teachers perceived that school principals practiced CAL-SP as measured by the CAL-SPS.

ANOVA and t-tests were used to determine whether there are significant differences among CAL-SP dimensions and the individual demographics of schoolteachers including their gender, length of service (LoS), age, and union membership.

Sample and Data Collection

Our study population consisted of a total of 1,203 public-schoolteachers; they were then divided into a stratified random sampling from secondary schools in Eskisehir, Turkey. In this procedure, the population was divided into subgroups on the basis of a variable chosen by researchers. Once the population was divided, samples were drawn randomly from each subgroup (McMillan and Schumacher, 2006).

The schools were stratified according to TEOG exam results, namely, their academic success level was divided into high-achieving, middle-achieving, and low-achieving schools. TEOG is a type of selection and placement examination given to students before the transition to high school from eighth grade; in other words, the completion of primary education and the beginning of secondary education.

The scores of the students obtained from the TEOG examination determine the high schools in which they will be placed, so it is a very important examination. It is a central selection, placement examination system that is given by the Ministry of National Education twice a year on two dates (six exams each). For our study, equal-sized samples were randomly selected from all public schools. According to Gay and Airasian (2000), "equal-sized samples would be the most useful if you want to compare the performance of different subgroups."

A total of 424 schoolteachers were analyzed in this research. The data-collection method was a self-administered, paper-based questionnaire. Questionnaires were distributed to participants at their schools for completion at their own convenience to provide them with anonymity. Data gained from the returned questionnaires indicated that the majority of the teachers were female ($n = 291$, 68.6 percent); male participation was ($n = 133$, 31.4 percent).

Instrumentation

The survey instrument used in this study was CAL-SP (Ozen and Turan 2017). The CAL-SP was designed to measure leadership qualities. It consists of two components: the demographic section and CAL-SPS, a forty-five-item Likert-scale questionnaire, which is a five-point ordinal scale (completely disagree, disagree, neutral, agree, and completely agree) measuring three areas of leadership skills: ML, AL, and EL. The questionnaire has shown high face validity and predictive validity, meaning that the results not only make sense to people but also predict the level of a leader's performance.

Reliability of the CAL-SP Scale was determined using test-retest reliability and Cronbach's coefficient alpha. Test-retest reliability for the three dimensions was at the 0.93 level or above. Computed coefficient alphas for each of the three leadership practices of CAL-SP in this study were ML (Cronbach's $\alpha = 0.94$), AL (Cronbach's $\alpha = 0.91$), and EL (Cronbach's $\alpha = 0.96$) (Ozen, 2015; Ozen and Turan, 2017).

RESULTS

The first research question addressed measured the perceptions of the teachers according to their clusters on the facets of the CAL-SP. Means and standards deviations were used to answer this question. Starting with the means, it is observable from table 3.1 that the lowest mean of practicing CAL-SP in cluster 1 was 2.98 with EL and the highest mean was 3.37 with AL; furthermore, the CAL-SP total was 3.19. In cluster 2, the lowest mean was 3.38 with EL, the highest level was 3.63 with AL. The CAL-SP total was 3.49. In cluster 3, the lowest value was 3.45 with EL, the highest level was 3.68 with AL. The CAL-SP total was 3.63.

The second research question concerned the significant differences among CAL-SP model dimensions and demographics of teachers' gender, LoS, age, and union membership. To examine the difference in means between males and female teachers in each dimension of CAL-SP Scale, t-tests for independent samples were used. However, the ANOVA was utilized to identify whether the variances in the length of service, age, and union membership were equal or significantly different.

Table 3.2 shows no significant differences between male and female teachers' perceptions in the ML dimension ($F = -0.90, p = 0.36$), AL dimension ($F = -1.25, p = 0.21$), EL dimension ($F = -1.57, p = 0.11$), nor CAL-SP total ($F = -0.90, p = 0.3$) in cluster 1, which were high-achieving schools.

Table 3.2 shows that there were no significant differences between male and female teachers in perceptions of principals' AL ($F = -2.19, p = 0.42$) or CAL-SP total ($F = -1.86, p = 0.06$). However, table 3.2 illustrates significant differences between male and female teachers' perceptions with regard to the ML ($F = -2.20, p = 0.02$) and EL ($F = -2.19, p = 0.03$) dimensions in cluster 2, which were middle-achieving schools. Female teachers obtained a mean score 3.36, male teachers obtained 3.64. The F-ratio was -2.02, which

Table 3.1. Means and Standard Deviations of the Overall and Each of the Three Dimensions of CAL-SP Scale

	Cluster 1 (N = 152)		Cluster 2 (N = 164)		Cluster 3 (N = 108)	
	Mean	SD	Mean	SD	Mean	SD
ML	3.09	0.95	3.45	0.76	3.60	0.70
AL	3.37	0.84	3.63	0.73	3.68	0.71
EL	2.98	0.99	3.38	0.71	3.45	0.76
CAL-SP TOTAL	3.19	0.87	3.49	0.68	3.62	0.63

Table 3.2. The Differences Between Male and Female Teachers in Each Dimension of CAL-SP

Dimensions	Gender	Cluster 1 (N = 152, (F = 124, M=28))			Cluster 2 (N = 164) (F = 111, M = 53)			Cluster 3 (N = 108) (F = 56, M = 52)		
		Mean	T	p	Mean	T	p	Mean	T	p
ML	F	3.05	-0.90	0.36	3.36	-2.20	0.02	3.43	-2.76	0.00
	M	3.24			3.64			3.79		
AL	F	3.33	-1.25	0.21	3.60	-0.79	0.42	3.53	-2.32	0.02
	M	3.56			3.70			3.84		
EL	F	2.92	-1.57	0.11	3.30	-2.19	0.03	3.30	-2.17	0.03
	M	3.25			3.55			3.61		
CAL-SP TOTAL	F	3.16	-0.90	0.36	3.42	-1.86	0.06	3.45	-3.01	0.00
	M	3.33			3.63			3.81		

showed that these two groups differed in their ML perceptions, since the F-ratio was statistically significant.

There were significant differences between male and female teachers' perceptions of principals' practices in the dimension of EL ($F = -2.19$, $p = 0.03$). Female teachers obtained a mean score 3.30, male teachers obtained 3.55. The F-ratio was -2.19, which showed that these two groups were different in their EL perceptions, since the F-ratio was statistically significant.

Furthermore, there were significant differences between male and female teachers' perceptions in the ML ($F = -2.76$, $p = 0.00$), AL ($F = -2.32$, $p = 0.02$), EL ($F = -2.17$, $p = 0.03$), and CAL-SP total ($F = -3.01$, $p = 0.00$) dimensions in cluster 3, which were the lowest-achieving schools. Female teachers obtained a mean score 3.43, male teachers obtained 3.79. The F-ratio was -2.76, which showed that these two groups differed in their ML perceptions, since the F-ratio was statistically significant.

Female teachers obtained a mean score 3.53, male teachers obtained 3.84. The F-ratio was -2.32, which showed that these two groups differed in their AL perceptions, since the F-ratio was statistically significant.

Female teachers obtained a mean score 3.30, male teachers obtained 3.61. The F-ratio was -2.17, which showed that these two groups differed in their ML perceptions, since the F-ratio was statistically significant.

Female teachers obtained a mean score 3.45, male teachers obtained 3.81. The F-ratio was -3.01, which showed that these two groups differed in their CAL-SP total perceptions, since the F-ratio was statistically significant.

On the other hand, table 3.3 shows the differences of teachers' perceptions based on LoS of teachers among the six groups in all three clusters. In cluster 1, which was the high-achieving schools, there were no significant differences between the six LoS groups with regard to the dimensions of ML ($F = 1.78$, $p = 0.11$), AL ($F = 2.23$, $p = 0.08$), EL ($F = 2.77$, $p = 0.07$), or CAL-SP total ($F = 2.13$, $p = 0.06$).

However, cluster 2 showed differences between groups with regard to each dimension and CAL-SP total. In other words, there were significant differences between the six LoS groups with regard to the dimension of ML ($F = 5.02$, $p = 0.00$). Teachers who had six to ten years LoS showed difference from the teachers who had eleven to fifteen years, sixteen to twenty years, and more than twenty-six years of LoS.

Teachers who had six to ten years of LoS got a mean score of 3.11, teachers who had eleven to fifteen years of LoS scored 3.59, teachers who had sixteen to twenty years of LoS scored 3.65, teachers who had more than twenty-six years LoS scored 3.95. The F-ratio is 5.02, which shows that these six groups differ with regard to LoS variables, since the F-ratio is statistically significant.

There were significant differences between the six LoS groups with regard to the dimension of AL ($F = 3.92$, $p = 0.02$). Teachers who had six to ten years LoS showed difference from the teachers who had eleven to fifteen years and sixteen to twenty years, and more than twenty-six years LoS. Teachers who had six to ten years LoS got a mean score of 3.32, teachers who had eleven to fifteen years of LoS scored 3.77, teachers who had sixteen to twenty years LoS scored 3.90, teachers who had more than twenty-six years LoS scored 3.93. The F-ratio is 3.92, which shows that these six groups differ with regard to LoS variables, since the F-ratio is statistically significant.

We found significant differences between the six LoS groups with regard to the dimension of EL ($F = 3.45$, $p = 0.00$). Teachers who had six to ten years LoS showed difference from the teachers who had more than twenty-six years LoS. Teachers who had six to ten years of LoS got a mean score of 3.34, teachers who had more than twenty-six years LoS scored 3.91. The F-ratio is 3.45, which shows that these six groups differ with regard to LoS variables, since the F-ratio is statistically significant.

There were also significant differences found between the six LoS groups with regard to the dimension of CAL-SP total ($F = 4.54$, $p = 0.01$). Teachers who had six to ten years LoS showed difference with regard to the teachers who had sixteen to twenty years and those with more than twenty-six years LoS. Teachers who had six to ten years LoS got a mean score of 3.26, teachers who had sixteen to twenty years LoS scored 3.82, teachers who had more than twenty-six years LoS scored 3.93. The F-ratio is 4.54, which shows that these six groups differ with regard to LoS variables, since the F-ratio is statistically significant.

Table 3.3. The Differences among the LoS of Teachers in Each Dimension of CAL-SP (Cluster 1-2-3)

	LoS	Cluster 1 (N=152)						Cluster 2 (N=164)						Cluster 3 (N=108)					
		N	Mean	sd	F	p	MD	N	Mean	sd	F	p	MD	N	Mean	sd	F	p	MD
ML	1–5	16	2.86	0.74	1.78	0.11	–	10	3.13	0.87	5.02	0.00	B-C	18	3.44	0.87	0.50	0.76	–
	6–10	33	3.48	0.98				52	3.11	0.78			B-D	20	3.62	0.75			
	11–15	32	3.03	0.96				47	3.59	0.60			B-F	28	3.54	0.60			
	16–20	39	3.09	0.86				25	3.65	0.70				28	3.73	0.75			
	21–25	14	2.84	1.3				14	3.54	0.76				5	3.75	0.40			
	26+	16	2.82	0.79				16	3.95	0.71				7	3.74	0.30			
AL	1–5	16	3.15	0.63	2.23	0.08	–	10	3.41	0.78	3.92	0.00	B-C	18	3.59	0.85	0.45	0.08	–
	6–10	33	3.75	0.81				52	3.32	0.77			B-D	20	3.67	0.76			
	11–15	32	3.32	0.89				47	3.77	0.59			B-F	28	3.72	0.60			
	16–20	39	3.38	0.72				25	3.90	0.56				28	3.81	0.70			
	21–25	14	3.19	1.2				14	3.64	0.85				5	3.72	0.66			
	26+	16	3.05	0.73				16	3.93	0.71				7	3.21	0.77			
EL	1–5	16	2.58	0.86	2.7	0.07	–	10	3.63	0.88	3.45	0.00	B-F	18	3.44	0.67	0.26	0.93	–
	6–10	33	3.33	1.0				52	3.34	0.69				20	3.66	0.77			
	11–15	32	2.98	0.90				47	3.71	0.50				28	3.58	0.66			
	16–20	39	3.06	0.87				25	3.90	0.63				28	3.70	0.75			
	21–25	14	2.87	1.4				14	3.69	0.74				5	3.39	0.39			
	26+	16	2.55	0.85				16	3.91	0.83				7	3.59	0.21			

LoS	Cluster 1 (N=152)						Cluster 2 (N=164)						Cluster 3 (N=108)					
	N	Mean	sd	F	p	MD	N	Mean	sd	F	p	MD	N	Mean	sd	F	p	MD
CAL-SP TOT 1–5	16	2.95	0.71	2.13	0.06	–	10	3.39	0.80	4.54	0.00	B-D	18	0.75	0.17	0.37	0.86	–
6–10	33	3.57	0.89				52	3.26	0.70			B-F	20	0.66	0.14			
11–15	32	3.14	0.87				47	3.69	0.52				28	0.57	0.10			
16–20	39	3.23	0.78				25	3.82	0.59				28	0.70	0.13			
21–25	14	2.98	1.2				14	3.62	0.77				5	0.47	0.21			
26+	16	2.88	0.66				16	3.93	0.71				7	0.31	0.11			

In cluster 3, there were no significant differences between the six groups with regard to each dimension of CAL-SP scale. In other words, no significant differences were found between the six LoS groups with regard to the dimension of ML ($F = 0.50$, $p = 0.76$), AL ($F = 0.45$, $p = 0.08$), EL ($F = 0.26$, $p = 0.93$), or CAL-SP total ($F = 0.37$, $p = 0.86$).

Table 3.4 shows the differences in age of teachers among the four groups in all three clusters. In cluster 1, which was the high-achieving schools, there were no significant differences among the four age groups in any dimension of the CAL-SP scale. In other words, we found no significant differences between the four age groups with regard to the dimensions of ML ($F = 0.52$, $p = 0.66$), AL ($F = 1.07$, $p = 0.36$), EL ($F = 1.09$, $p = 0.35$), and CAL-SP total ($F = 0.99$, $p = 0.39$).

However, cluster 2 showed differences with regard to the ML dimension. In other words, there were significant differences between the four age groups with regard to the dimension of ML ($F = 4.13$, $p = 0.00$). Teachers who were under thirty years of age showed difference from teachers who were between forty-one and fifty years old. Teachers under thirty got a mean score of 3.14, forty-one- to fifty-year-old teachers got a mean score of 3.63. The F-ratio is 4.13, which shows that these four groups differ with regard to age variables, since the F-ratio is statistically significant.

Also, there were significant differences between the four age groups with regard to the dimension of AL ($F = 3.20$, $p = 0.02$). Teachers under thirty years of age showed difference from teachers who were between forty-one and fifty years old. Teachers under thirty got a mean score of 3.33, forty-one- to fifty-year-old teachers got a mean score of 3.83. The F-ratio is 3.20, which shows that these four groups differ with regard to age variables, since the F-ratio is statistically significant.

There were no significant differences among the four levels of age groups in the dimensions of EL ($F = 2.28$, $p = 0.08$), or CAL-SP total ($F = 3.40$, $p = 0.19$).

In cluster 3, we found no significant differences among the four age groups in any dimension of the CAL-SP scale. In other words, in cluster 3 there were no significant differences between the four levels of age groups with regard to the dimensions of ML ($F = 1.09$, $p = 0.35$), AL ($F = 1.62$, $p = 0.19$), EL ($F = 0.70$, $p = 0.54$), or CAL-SP total ($F = 1.24$, $p = 0.30$).

Table 3.5 shows the differences of union membership of teachers among the five groups in all three clusters. In cluster 1, no significant differences were found among the five groups with regard to each dimension of the CAL-SP scale. In other words, there were no significant differences between the five union-membership groups with regard to the dimension of ML ($F = 0.49$, $p = 0.74$), AL ($F = 0.37$, $p = 0.82$), EL ($F = 1.01$, $p = 0.40$), or CAL-SP total ($F = 0.53$, $p = 0.73$). However, cluster 2 showed differences with regard to each dimension and the CAL-SP total.

Table 3.4. The Differences among the Age of Teachers in Each Dimensions of CAL-SP (Cluster 1-2-3)

	Age	Cluster 1 (N=152)						Cluster 2 (N=164)						Cluster 3 (N=108)					
		N	Mean	sd	F	p	MD	N	Mean	sd	F	p	MD	N	Mean	sd	F	p	MD
ML	30 below	28	3.20	0.85	0.52	0.66	-	33	3.14	0.74	4.13	0.00	A-C	26	3.42	0.79	1.09	0.35	-
	31–40	63	3.14	0.98				86	3.44	0.76				41	3.62	0.74			
	41–50	49	2.95	1.01				33	3.63	0.72				28	3.77	0.62			
	50 upper	10	3.05	0.75				12	3.91	0.64				8	3.60	0.48			
AL	30 below	28	3.47	0.73	1.0	0.36	-	33	3.33	0.73	3.20	0.02	A-C	26	3.48	0.81	1.62	0.19	-
	31–40	63	3.47	0.86				86	3.64	0.71				41	3.78	0.70			
	41–50	49	3.20	0.90				33	3.83	0.69				28	3.81	0.62			
	50 upper	10	3.31	0.69				12	3.86	0.70				8	3.41	0.71			
EL	30 below	28	3.19	0.93	1.0	0.35		33	3.40	0.67	2.28	0.08	-	26	3.43	0.76	0.70	0.54	-
	31–40	63	3.23	0.98				86	3.64	0.66				41	3.66	0.72			
	41–50	49	2.92	1.0				33	3.83	0.71				28	3.65	0.62			
	50 upper	10	3.29	0.45				12	3.69	0.80				8	3.50	0.32			
CAL-SP	30 below	28	3.29	0.80	0.99	0.39	-	33	3.29	0.67	3.40	0.19	-	26	3.44	0.69	1.24	0.30	-

	Age	Cluster 1 (N=152)						Cluster 2 (N=164)						Cluster 3 (N=108)					
		N	Mean	sd	F	p	MD	N	Mean	sd	F	p	MD	N	Mean	sd	F	p	MD
TOT	31–40	64	3.29	0.88				86	3.58	0.66				41	3.69	0.67			
	41–50	50	3.02	0.93				33	3.76	0.67				28	3.74	0.58			
	50 upper	10	3.22	0.50				12	3.82	0.69				8	3.50	0.36			

Table 3.5. The Differences among the Membership Union of Teachers in Each Dimensions of CAL-SP (Cluster 1-2-3)

	UNIONS	Cluster 1 (N=152)						Cluster 2 (N=164)						Cluster 3 (N=108)					
		N	Mean	sd	F	p	MD	N	Mean	sd	F	p	MD	N	Mean	sd	F	p	MD
ML	Lefist Democrat	12	2.89	0.84	0.49	0.74	-	26	3.40	0.74	0.35	0.00	B-D	15	3.33	1.02	1.33	0.00	C-A
	Right-Wing	31	3.23	1.09				21	3.58	0.95				24	3.61	0.71			
	Center Nationalist	18	3.24	1.06				47	3.52	0.67				13	3.97	0.59			
	Leftist Nationalist	5	2.74	0.91				11	3.39	0.96				12	3.53	0.62			
	Other	9	3.23	0.88				13	3.31	0.84				7	3.51	0.60			
AL	Lefist Democrat	12	3.31	0.73	0.37	0.85	-	26	3.64	0.68	0.42	0.02	B-D	15	3.39	1.06	2.32	0.00	C-A
	Right-Wing	31	3.54	1.01				21	3.77	0.98				24	3.76	0.68			
	Center Nationalist	18	3.40	0.93				47	3.55	0.59				13	4.21	0.48			
	Leftist Nationalist	5	3.14	0.65				11	3.67	0.94				12	3.70	0.52			
	Other	9	3.51	0.65				13	3.47	0.97				7	3.50	0.85			
EL	Lefist Democrat	12	3.08	0.86	1.01	0.40	-	26	3.62	0.60	0.83	0.04	C-D	15	3.35	0.97	0.96	0.00	C-D
	Right-Wing	31	3.20	0.98				21	3.66	0.88				24	3.73	0.65			

	UNIONS	Cluster 1 (N=152)						Cluster 2 (N=164)						Cluster 3 (N=108)					
		N	Mean	sd	F	p	MD	N	Mean	sd	F	p	MD	N	Mean	sd	F	p	MD
	Center Nationalist	18	3.46	1.01				47	3.69	0.55				13	3.79	0.51			
	Leftist Nationalist	5	2.49	1.29				11	3.60	0.80				12	3.68	0.70			
	Other	9	3.09	1.01				13	3.47	0.90				7	3.48	0.47			
CAL-SP TOT	Leftist Democrat	12	3.09	0.75	0.53	0.73	-	26	3.55	0.64	0.37	0.04	C-A	15	3.36	0.95	1.65	0.00	C-A
	Right-Wing	31	3.33	1.00				21	3.67	0.92				24	3.70	0.63			
	Center Nationalist	18	3.37	0.94				47	3.58	0.54				13	3.99	0.47			
	Leftist Nationalist	5	2.79	0.92				11	3.55	0.88				12	3.63	0.58			
	Other	9	3.27	0.80				13	3.42	0.87				7	3.49	0.49			

In cluster 2, there were significant differences between the five union-membership groups with regard to the dimension of ML ($F = 0.35$, $p = 0.00$). Teachers who were members to the leftist nationalist union (Eğitim-Is), which opposes the party holding political power, showed difference from the teachers who were members of the right-wing union (Eğitim-Bir-Sen), which is on the side of the party holding political power. Teachers who were members of Eğitim-Bir-Sen got a mean score of 3.58, while teachers who were members of Eğitim-Is got a mean score of 3.39. The F-ratio is 0.35, which shows that these five groups differ with regard to the union-membership variable, since the F-ratio is statistically significant.

There were significant differences between the five union-membership groups with regard to the dimension of AL ($F = 0.42$, $p = 0.02$). Teachers who were members of Eğitim-Bir-Sen got a mean score of 3.77, while teachers who were members of Eğitim-Is got a mean score of 3.67. The F-ratio is 0.42, which shows that these five groups differ with regard to the union-membership variable, since the F-ratio is statistically significant.

There were significant differences between the five union-membership groups with regard to the dimension of EL ($F = 0.83$, $p = 0.04$). Teachers who were members of Eğitim-Sen, which opposes the party currently holding political power, showed difference from teachers who were members of Eğitim-Bir-Sen. Teachers who were members of Eğitim-Bir-Sen got a mean score of 3.66, while Eğitim-Sen union members got a mean score of 3.62. The F-ratio is 0.83, which shows that these five groups differ with regard to the union-membership variable, since F-ratio is statistically significant.

There were significant differences between the five union-membership groups with regard to the dimension of CAL-SP total ($F = 0.37$, $p = 0.04$). Teachers who were members of Eğitim-Is showed difference from teachers who were members of the right wing union Eğitim-Bir-Sen. Teachers who were members of Eğitim-Bir-Sen got a mean score of 3.67, while teachers who were members of Eğitim-Is got a mean score of 3.55. The F-ratio is 0.37, which shows that these five groups differ with regard to the union-membership variable, since the F-ratio is statistically significant.

In cluster 3, there were significant differences between the five union-membership groups with regard to the dimension of ML ($F = 1.33$, $p = 0.00$). Teachers who were members to center nationalist union (TEMSEN) showed difference from teachers who were members Eğitim-Sen. Teachers who were members of TEMSEN got a mean score of 3.97, while teahers who were members of Eğitim-Sen got a mean score of 3.33. The F-ratio is 1.33, which shows that these five groups differ with regard to the union-membership variable, since the F-ratio is statistically significant.

Significant differences were found between the five union-membership groups with regard to the dimension of AL ($F = 2.32$, $p = 0.00$). Teachers who were members of TEMSEN showed difference from teachers who were members of Eğitim-Sen. Teachers who were members of TEMSEN got a mean score of 4.21, while teachers who were members of Eğitim-Sen got a mean score of 3.39. The F-ratio is 2.32, which shows that these five groups differ with regard to the union-membership variable, since the F-ratio is statistically significant.

We found significant differences between the five union-membership groups with regard to the dimension of EL ($F = 0.96$, $p = 0.00$). Teachers who were members of TEMSEN showed difference from teachers who were members of Eğitim-Is. Teachers who were members of TEMSEN got a mean score of 3.79, while teachers who were members of Eğitim-Is got a mean score of 3.68. The F-ratio is 0.96, which shows that these five groups differ with regard to the union-membership variable, since the F-ratio is statistically significant.

Significant differences were found between the five union-membership groups in the dimension of CAL-SP total ($F = 1.65$, $p = 0.00$). Teachers who were members of TEMSEN showed difference from teachers who were members of Eğitim-Sen. Teachers who were members of TEMSEN got a mean score of 3.99, while teachers who were members of Eğitim-Sen got a mean score of 3.36. The F-ratio is 1.65, which shows that these five groups differ with regard to the union-membership variable, since the F-ratio is statistically significant.

CONCLUSION

In recent years, there has been a growth in the number of articles, studies, dissertations, and academic research in the area of leadership. In Turkey, several theories and models, and their respective measurement instruments, have been developed and used to measure leadership behaviors. However, CT and CAL are newly blossoming theories. It is difficult to find a practice on CAL except Obolensky's (2010) research and practice.

This study was the first in a school context to practice and model the CAL-SP model from the lens of CT. Therefore, the purpose of this study was to examine, in practice, the CAL-SP model in Turkish schools as perceived by teachers. Results such as those in this study might point to a substantial gap in understanding the influence of societal culture and context on CAL-SP. This study filled the gap struggling to apply new theories, namely CT, attempting to understand the phenomena (Ozen and Turan, 2017).

The findings revealed that the CAL-SP model in Turkish schools was practiced moderately, and showed that teachers at high-achieving schools perceived their principals' CAL-SP practices at less than those at medium- and low-achieving schools. The success of high-achieving schools did not stem from the leadership skills of school principals; it was likely based on the fact that students' families' socioeconomic level was high, and role of family was greater than the role of principals and teachers. Aksoy (2018) also revealed that families who had high income and high education levels spent more money for their children's education because the educational system was challenging and test-based.

Another reason for the low perceptions of schoolteachers on their school principals' leadership skills is that most schoolteachers are aware that the centralized system paralyzes the functions of school principals. This finding was supported also by Lindquist (2017), purporting that the strict centralized educational system existed in Turkey.

The more teachers demand, the more school principals fall short in meeting expectations because decisions and budgets are made centrally from the Ministry of National Education (MoNE). Thus, teachers meet the needs of extra educational materials and test books for their students from students' families, not from the school management, which might decrease the CAL-SP functions of school principals.

As for low-achieving schools, teachers perceived the CAL-SP practices in the highest level in this study. The families of these schools belonged to a low socioeconomic level, so they were not as assertive or determined that their children would succeed. Teachers also did not demand much from families, students, and their principals. Principals reciprocally also did not demand much from their teachers.

This mutual interaction created a consensus between teachers and principals that neither teachers nor principals forced each other to enable the students to succeed. There were no satisfying efforts from any side: families, teachers, or school principals. Whatever school principals did, it seemed to schoolteachers to be a big action because resources were scarce.

From different perspectives, it might be claimed that teachers teaching at middle- and low-achieving schools are aware of the fact that education is the only way to rescue those children whose families have middle and low incomes from the low-income trap. For that reason, academic resilience might occur among these teachers. Middle- and low-achieving schools lacked educational and physical materials. Teachers and school principals showed great efforts to increase the success of children in a complex adaptive school environment, not expecting much from the families and state.

According to the CAL-SP perceptions of the teachers working in high-achieving schools, there was no significant difference in ML, AL, EL, or CAL-SP total scores regarding the gender variable. There was a significant difference in the ML dimension of the middle-achieving schools in that male teachers perceived the ML practice in principals more than female teachers did. In low-achieving schools, male teachers perceived ML, Al, EL, and CAL-SP practices more than female teachers did.

Based on the results obtained from this research, it can be conceived first that discriminative behavior based on gender identity toward female teachers in schools might cause significant difference in ML perceptions in middle-achieving schools and on all dimensions, including CAL-SP total, in low-achieving schools (Dogramaci, 2000). The two genders are already experiencing tensions in educational contexts because gender roles marginalize females in secular-anti secular, traditional-modern line so access, presentation, and limitation of women's educational opportunities are still reinforced by traditional patriarchal structures.

This finding could be seen to show that Islamism has grown as a response to social, economic, education, and political discontent in Turkey, including foreign influences, urbanization, modernization, and secularization. The Islamist movement's upsurge, the growth of ultra-nationalism, and Kurdish ethno-nationalism has eroded the center in Turkey. The center-right parties have declined because they did not meet their constituency's needs or expectations, and also failed to absorb the compromising spirit of democratic identity parting the human male-female, secular-anti-secular (Narli, 1999).

Another reason may be that female teachers in middle- and low-achieving schools have higher expectations within the teaching and education field than male teachers. Education is seen as an important means of destroying class differences and empowering women in society (Luttrell, 1997).

According to the perceptions of the teachers who worked in the high- and low-achieving schools, there was no significant difference regarding LoS in ML, AL, EL, and CAL-SP total scores. However, there was a significant difference in the perceptions of the teachers at middle-achieving schools on their school principals' ML, AL, and EL practices. The teachers who had been teaching for six to eleven years perceived the ML, AL, EL, and CAL-SP total less than the other teachers who had longer LoS.

This can be expressed as the failure of the school principals to meet the expectations of young teachers. In research related to the Turkish education system, the centralized structure neglected the urgent requirements of teachers and school partners and limited the creativity of young and eligible teachers, causing ineffective schools and demotivated teachers (Turan et al., 2010). The Turkish educational system must change the centralized management that affects teacher effectiveness, student success, motivation, and the spirit of innovation of young teachers (Ashton and Webb, 1986).

Another finding was that teachers in middle- and low-achieving schools who were members of unions opposing the current political party in power perceived ML, AL, EL, and CAL-SP total scores to be lower than did the teachers who were members of the unions that were aligned with the political party in power. Right-wing unions took the side of the political party in power in Turkey.

Yet, it had a great power from determining the educational policies to assigning the school principals and teachers. Merit and skill were not required, being a member would be enough, instead. It might be claimed that there is a clash between teachers and principals who were the member of different unions. Principals might favor the teachers who were the member of the same union while discriminating against the others.

Success in many facets of life is based not on merit but on mutual friendships and cronyism (Inal, 2012). This has been especially true of the education system in Turkey (Aydogan, 2009). Also, the nomination and selection processes of school principals have been problematic (Baydar, 2005; Aybek, 2017).

LIMITATIONS AND FUTURE DIRECTIONS

This study used the quantitative method of survey design, which has some limitations worth mentioning. First, teachers' answers in the study were fairly succinct, not in-depth. This could be due to the nature of the research methodology of quantitative studies. It has long been acknowledged that CT is a challenge to determinism, but a quantitative method was used, which is a strict deterministic approach.

Future research can use certain techniques or second-order scientific methods to have teachers elaborate on their perceptions of CAL-SP practices. This could be done by qualitative research, fuzzy logic, or meta-analyses. The sample diversity could also be expanded by recruiting teachers from other regions of Turkey, as each region has its own characteristics that may affect teachers' CAL-SP perceptions.

REFERENCES

Aksoy, H. (2018). *Educational expenditures of families*. Unpublished master project, Pamukkale Universitesi Egitim Bilimleri Enstitüsü.

Aybek, S. (2017). *The mistake of the millennium: Appointment of the vice-school principals by interview*. http://www.egitimajansi.com/sahin-aybek/ceyrek-yuzyilin-egitim-hatasi-mulakatla-mudur-yardimcisi-atamak-kose-yazisi-863y.html.

Aydın, A. (2015). *The politics of education*. Ankara: PEGEM.

Aydogan, I. (2009). Favoritism in the Turkish educational system: Nepotism, cronyism and patronage. *Eğitimde Politika Analizleri ve Stratejik Arastirmalar Dergisi, 4* (1), 19–35.

Baydar, T. (2005). Yönetim etigine genel bir bakis [Introduction to administrative ethics]. *Turk Administration Journal, 449*, 47–74.

Bedeian, A. G., and Hunt, J. G. (2006). Academic amnesia and vestigial assumptions of our forefathers. *The Leadership Quarterly, 17*(2), 190–205.

Birkinshaw, J., Bouquet, C., and Barsoux, J. (2011). The 5 myths of innovation. *MIT Sloan Management Review, 52*(2), 43–50.

Burnes, B. (2005). Complexity theories and organizational change. *International Journal of Management Reviews, 7* (2), 73–90.

Chaffee, E. E. (1983). *Rational decision making in higher education*. Denver, CO: National Center for Higher Education Management Systems.

Dogramaci, E. (2000). *Women in Turkey and the new millennium*. Ankara: Ataturk Research Center.

Dougherty, D., and Hardy, C. (1996). Sustained product innovation in large, mature organizations: Overcoming innovation-to-organization problems. *Academy of Management Journal, 39*, 1120−153.

Fullan, M. G. (1992). Getting reform right: What works and what doesn't. *Phi Delta Kappa, 73*(10), 744–52.

Ford, R. (2010). Complex adaptive leading-ship and open-processional change processes. *Leadership and Organization Development Journal, 31* (5), 420–35.

Gay, L. R., and Airasian, P. (2000). *Educational research: Competencies for analysis and application* (6th ed.). NJ: Prentice-Hall.

Heifetz, R. A. (1994). *Leadership without easy answers*. Cambridge, MA: Harvard University Press.

Inal, K. (2012). AKP'nin reform mantığı ve '4+4+4' ün ideo-pedagojik eleştirel analizi [The AKP's Logic of reform and its critical politico-ideologicalanalysis in terms of new noncontinuous education law]. *Eğitim Bilim Toplum, 10*(39), 78–92.

Jehn, K. A. (1997). A qualitative analysis of conflict types and dimensions in organizational groups. *Administrative Science Quarterly, 42*, 530–57.

Johnson, S. (1996). *Leading to change: The challenge of the new superintendency*. San Francisco, CA: Jossey-Bass.

Jones, M., and Paterson, L. (1992). *Preventing chaos in times of crisis: A guide for school administrators*. Los Alamitos, CA: Southwest Regional Laboratory.

Koopmans, M. (2015). A dynamical view of high school attendance: An assessment of short-term and long-term dependencies in five urban schools. *Nonlinear Dynamics, Psychology and Life Sciences, 19*, 65–80.

Leithwood, K. (2001). Five reasons why most accountability policies don't work (and what you can do about it). *Orbit, 32*(1), 1–5.

Lindquist, C. (2017). Educational reform in Turkey. *International Journal of Progressive Education, 13*(2), 133–43.

Luttrell, W. (1997). *School-smart and Mother-wise*. New York, NY: Routledge.

McMillan, J. H., and Schumacher, S. (2006). *Research in education: Evidence-based inquiry* (6th ed.). Boston, MA: Allyn and Bacon.

Morin, E. (1999). *Seven complex lessons in education for the future*. Paris, France: UNESCO.

Mumford, M. D., Scott, G. M., Gaddis, B., and Strange, J. M. (2002). Leading creative people: Orchestrating expertise and relationships. *The Leadership Quarterly, 13*(6), 705–50.

Narli, N. (1999). The rise of the Islamist movement in Turkey. *Middle East Review of International Affairs, 3*(3), 38–48.

Obolensky, N. (2010). *Complex adaptive leadership: Embracing paradox and uncertainty*. New York, NY: Taylor & Francis.

Ozen, H. (2015). *The effect of motivational language used by school principals upon characteristics of complex adaptive leadership*. Unpublished doctoral dissertation, Eskisehir Osmangazi University Educational Sciences Institute, Turkey.

Ozen, H., and Turan, S. (2017). Scale development and initial tests of the multidimensional complex adaptive leadership scale for school principals: An exploratory mixed method study. *European Journal of Education Studies, 3*(12), 37–74.

Patton, M. Q. 2011. *Developmental evaluation: Applying complexity concepts to enhance innovation and use*. New York, NY: Guilford Press.

Schlechty, P. C. (2001). *Shaking up the school house: How to support and sustain educational innovation*. London, England: Jossey-Bass.

Turan, S., Yucel, C., Karatas E., and Demirhan, G. (2010). Okul mudurlerinin yerinden yonetim hakkındaki gorusleri [The perceptions of school principals on decentralized governance]. *Usak Universitesi Sosyal Bilimler Dergisi* [*Usak University Social Sciences Journal*], *3*(1), 1–18.

Turkoglu, P. (2000). *Tonguc ve enstituleri [Tonguc and his institutes]*. İstanbul, Turkey: Turkiye Is Bankasi Kultur yayinlari [Turkiye Is Bank Culture Publications].

Uhl-Bien, M., Marion, R., and McKelvey, B. (2007). Complexity leadership theory: Shifting leadership from the industrial age to the knowledge era. *The Leadership Quarterly, 18(4),* 298–318.

Yukl, G. (2010). *Leadership in organizations.* Upper Saddle River, NJ: Prentice Hall.

Yukl, G., and Mahsud, R. (2010). Why flexible and adaptive leadership is essential. *Consulting Psychology Journal: Research and Practice, 62,* 81–93.

Weick, K. (1969). *The social psychology of organizing.* Reading, MA: Addison-Wesley.

Chapter Four

Developing Great Educational Leaders

The Ontario College Experience

David A. Veres and Holly Catalfamo

The need for effective leadership in education has never been more important. The competition for scarce resources is at an all-time high while, at the same time, the demand for improved quality of education and educational service is becoming increasingly complex (Wallin, 2010). In addition, as the baby boom generation ages toward retirement, many educational leaders are leaving their posts, leaving a gap in leadership of a significant magnitude (Catalfamo, 2009; Wheeler, 2012).

Talented educators with potential to move into leadership roles seem uninterested or unmotivated to move into management positions within educational institutions (Cloud, 2010; Veres, 2016b; White, 2013). The educational institutions themselves often do not foster environments or cultures that value educational leaders (Veres, 2016b). There is also a noticeable lack of leader development available that would serve to fill the leadership pipeline in a systematic way (Catalfamo, 2009).

The described phenomenon likely represents many educational institutions in the United States and Canada at any level of education, including K–12 and postsecondary; however, this chapter explores the phenomenon of educational leadership in the Canadian context within the postsecondary environment, specifically Ontario community colleges. It provides a glimpse into the leadership development challenges and opportunities in the Ontario college system, which many will find relevant in jurisdictions around the world.

The chapter begins by describing the issues, concerns, and context of leadership and leader development within the Ontario college system. The Model of Educational Leader Development is introduced. This model examines the factors that motivate leaders and leader development as well as the factors that influence leader motivation and satisfaction in the work environment. The model illustrates how motivational factors and the work environment intersect with leader development opportunities to influence the acquisition of leadership skills, abilities, and competencies.

Utilizing the Model of Educational Leader Development, the chapter explores best practices in leadership development that may have application across all levels of education. By sharing specific examples of effective leadership development, insight is gained into how educational institutions have developed organizational cultures that foster leader recognition and promote effective leadership development.

CONTEXT – THE COLLEGE LANDSCAPE IN CANADA

Colleges are a relatively new phenomenon in Canada in comparison to university institutions, which have existed for well over a century (Catalfamo, 2009). During the late 1960s, a system of twenty-two colleges was created (Skolnik, 2002) during a period of unprecedented growth and expansion in postsecondary education (Dennison and Levin, 1989). At present, there are twenty-four publicly funded colleges in Ontario.

Given the rapid pace of change in education influenced by the impact of globalization (Levin, 1999), colleges are facing significant challenges that require educational leaders to have the competencies required to lead change, provide vision, and demonstrate stewardship for their colleges as they move through the turbulent twenty-first century. Thus, it could be argued that the need for developing leadership competencies has never been more pressing (Catalfamo, 2009).

When reviewing the literature related to leadership development within Ontario colleges, it is apparent that, although most colleges seem to recognize that human resources development is an important issue (Dennison and Levin, 1989), there is little uniformity across the system in terms of the strategies employed by colleges to address the leadership development challenge (Polonsky, 2003). There are formal educational programs that are offered nationally by well-recognized organizations, such as the Higher Education PhD offered within the Department of Leadership, Higher and Adult Education at the Ontario Institute for Studies in Education (OISE) at the University of Toronto.

Additionally, the national advocacy organization for colleges, Colleges and Institutes Canada, provides valuable senior leadership development through the National Executive Leadership Institute for Prospective Presidents (NELI) and the National Executive Leadership Institute for Prospective Vice-Presidents (VPNELI). However, for those more junior in their careers considered to be developing or emerging leaders, there is still much work to do by way of creating a meaningful and comprehensive approach to leader development.

Despite the plethora of conferences, workshops, and seminars that individuals can attend to network, exchange ideas, and obtain pieces of the huge leadership puzzle, individuals who are considering moving into leadership positions within colleges are unlikely to encounter a systematic, developmental program that meets their individual needs as future organizational leaders (Veres, 2016b).

ISSUES AND CONCERNS

The leadership development gap is an issue worthy of serious consideration as there are several factors that give rise to the awareness that educational institutions are facing a significant challenge as it relates to both recruiting and developing leaders. With an aging population in Canada and the United States, and most baby boomers at or approaching retirement age, there has been a significant loss of leadership talent (American Association of Community Colleges Leadership Suite, 2013; College Administrator, 2009).

At the same time, there seems to be little to motivate faculty to move into leadership roles, even though they seem the most natural successors. Extrinsic factors, such as pay, do not provide enough financial incentive for faculty to move into challenging administrative roles that are often characterized by role overload (Veres, 2016a). The collective agreement that governs all twenty-four public Ontario colleges restricts movement between management and faculty; once faculty move into an administrative position for more than twenty-four months, they are unable to return to teaching and retain their original seniority (College Employer Council and OPSEU, 2014).

Talented faculty often plateau in their careers at a coordinator level, which allows them informal academic leadership but sustains their position within the bargaining unit as professors. There is a lack of meaningful leadership development or succession planning available in most institutions (Veres, 2016b), which is troublesome for colleges at an individual level; it is equally problematic for the system as a whole. Boggs (2003) noted that leadership and faculty development institutes needed to do a better job of preparing individuals to meet the challenges of leadership. A decade and a half later, the challenge of leader development continues to be evident (Boggs, 2011).

It is also important to note that there is a lack of research focusing on community college leaders and leadership development within the Canadian context. However, there is a much broader base of literature in the United Sates (AACC Leadership Suite, 2013; Boggs, 2003, 2011; Cloud, 2010;

Cooper and Pagotto, 2003; Day, 2015; Duvall 2003; Leist and Travis, 2013; Piland and Wolf, 2003; Valeau and Boggs, 2004; Wheeler, 2012).

This chapter provides an opportunity to explore the Model of Educational Leader Development and share lessons learned from proactive institutions who are leading the charge with creative and meaningful leadership-development programming. This will enhance our understanding of those academic institutions providing innovative learning opportunities and interventions to develop the future leaders of their institutions.

MODEL OF EDUCATIONAL LEADERSHIP DEVELOPMENT

The Model of Educational Leadership Development was developed based on dissertation research conducted for "A Phenomenological Understanding of the Experience of Academic Administrators: Motivation, Satisfaction, Retention, and Succession Planning" (Veres, 2016b) and "An Examination of Leadership Development within Ontario's Colleges: Building Personal, Interpersonal, and Organizational Capacity" (Catalfamo, 2009).

The model provides a useful organizer to help explore the phenomenon of the development of college leaders. It includes the context of leader development, the motivating factors that impact college leaders, and the development opportunities that influence college leaders. Figure 4.1, The Model of Educational Leader Development, provides the visual representation of this conceptual framework.

At the center of the model is the educational leader. Educational leaders are motivated to pursue their careers in public service by a variety of factors, including a desire to serve their communities. Once becoming a member of the college community, they are immersed in a work environment that may support or negatively influence their satisfaction and their desire to take on leadership roles. The work environment also creates barriers to learning and development opportunities; the different types of learning to be explored include formal, nonformal, or informal learning. The following section will explore the model in greater detail.

Motivating Factors Affecting Academic Administrators

Understanding motivation is essential in both the development and recruitment of potential leaders, but also in the continued growth and advancement of existing leaders. Educational leaders demonstrate many of the characteristics associated with Public Sector Motivation (Anderfurhren-Biget, Varone, Giauque, and Ritz, 2010; Bright, 2013; Moynihan and Pandey, 2007; Perry and Hondeghem, 2008; Veres, 2016b), and these traits are often the reason they pursue this career path. Some individuals are motivated to service as a way of benefiting the broader community and are attracted to organizations

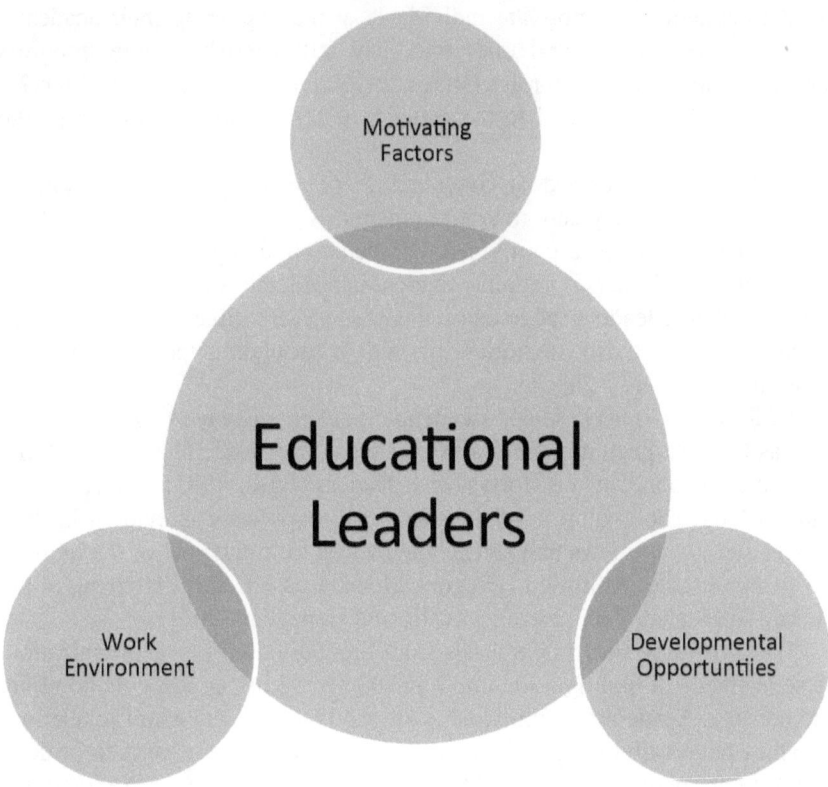

Figure 4.1. The Model of Educational Leader Development

such as educational institutions that have missions and values congruent with this focus.

Senior academic leaders are motivated by a myriad of factors in pursuing and continuing in these influential leadership roles. These individuals have a high degree of passion and concern for not only their institution's educational mission and vision but also that of the Ontario community college system. They are motivated by the benefits they provide to their students and their community. Throughout their growth within the Ontario community college system, they are acutely aware of the importance of a community college education to the citizenry of the province and its economic health (Veres, 2016b).

The main motivations for many academic leaders are centered on a sense of service. These academic leaders are motivated by the impact they had on supporting students in achieving their goals, assisting faculty and staff in providing a quality learning experience, and creating an environment in which the community can grow and prosper (Veres, 2016b). These outcomes are the elements that motivate individuals at the beginning their academic administrative careers, and ones that they still cherish as they progress through various leadership roles (Veres, 2016b). This commitment of service to others is directly related to the concept of servant leadership and public service motivation.

As originally described by Greenleaf (1977), servant leadership is about serving others, so they can grow and prosper. It is about ensuring that those who are less privileged are provided with benefit and opportunity. This focus on the growth of others is certainly evident in academic administrators. Many senior academic leaders reflected on their time as frontline academic administrator and it is those memories that aid in grounding their decisions as senior leaders (Veres, 2016b).

Additionally, many senior academic leaders displayed characteristics such as trust, respect, and admiration for those they lead. These characteristics are also found in transformational leaders (Bass, 1985; Veres, 2016b; Yukl, 2010). The evolution of their leadership approach is evident in their system and policy views that shifted their focus from the goal of the individual to that of the institution (Gregory Stone, Russell, and Patterson, 2004; Purkey and Siegel, 2003; Savage-Austin and Honeycutt, 2011).

Even with this shift in emphasis from the individual to the organization, these leaders still highlight the importance of integrity, ethics, collaboration, and honesty. Academic administrators are motivated by the working relationship they have with their peers and those they supervised and of their pride in how they are perceived by individuals in their institution and throughout the community. These traits are not only consistent with a servant leadership model, but also have been identified as essential ones for community college leaders (Boggs, 2003; Boroski, Buchsbaum, and Grief, 2009; de Guzman and Hapan, 2013; Eddy, 2012; Greenleaf, 1977; Veres, 2015).

Academic administrators are often values-driven and demonstrate a high degree of personal motivation and drive. As such, they are significantly influenced by the fit between themselves and the institution in which they serve (Veres, 2016b). These characteristics are well related to the concept of public service motivation (PSM). The influence of PSM seems to be more prevalent in managerial and supervisory staff (Christensen and Wright, 2011), which is well aligned with the focus of this research on academic administrators. The importance of a prosocial vision and mission, like those found in Ontario community colleges, is a strong attractor for those who demonstrate PSM traits (Bright, 2011; Christensen and Wright, 2011; Veres, 2016a: Wright, 2007).

Interestingly, the identified trend of existing academic leadership roles is also well aligned with the concept of PSM. Motivation and job satisfaction of individuals with PSM tend to decline as their tenure increases (Anderfurhren-

Biget et al., 2010; Bright, 2013). Although these individuals can be very tolerant of bureaucratic and structured environments, over time the existence of such internal and external barriers can wear at their prosocial motivation. This phenomenon, along with other environmental factors, may explain the trend of academic administrators switching institutions and even leaving postsecondary roles.

Factors Affecting the Academic Environment

Once in academic leadership roles, the level of motivation for these educational leaders is impacted by the environment in which they work. Barriers such as the bureaucratic nature of the institution, organizational culture, role clarity, a lack of recognition of the value of leaders, and the lack of leader development often negatively influence individual motivation and satisfaction (Veres, 2015; Veres, 2016b). These environmental factors can cause individuals to not seek out opportunities, leave institutions, or stay on as ineffective leaders (Veres, 2016b). Proactively working to mitigate these factors is essential for effective educational leader development to occur.

Job satisfaction, as well as professional and personal motivation, impact the future actions of academic leaders. Presently, leaders see more barriers than opportunities when looking at their place within the college leadership environment. Herzberg's (1982) two-factor theory involving intrinsic and extrinsic motivating components is commonly referenced when discussing postsecondary environments. A level of dissatisfaction amongst present and potential academic administrators has led to a demand for leaders that is challenging to meet (Palmer, 2013; Taylor, 2014; Veres, 2015).

The high stress of these leadership roles often leads individuals to question their sense of purpose and satisfaction (June, 2013; Veres, 2016b; White, 2013). This stress, as well as their respective lack of ability to maintain some level of work–life balance, has greatly influenced employment decisions. When frontline academic leaders feel abandoned in the "middle," they lose their motivation and desire to make a difference. It is the ability and drive to make things better that motivated them to take on these roles in the first place.

With ever increasingly complex leadership roles, individuals begin to question whether more senior roles are worth the challenges associated with those positions of authority (Veres, 2016b). Frontline academic leaders are pressured from the students they serve, the faculty they support, and the senior administration to whom they report. Within these environments, academic leaders face challenges associated with the fiscal realities of the postsecondary environment, changing client and community needs, and the demands to enhance program quality and delivery (Boggs, 2011; Cejda and Leist, 2013; Veres 2016b). This changing environment places new demands on academic administrators and situates them in new roles that require them to be constantly analyzing and designing new ways of delivering education (Bolman and Gallos, 2011).

The bureaucratic nature of the college environment is a common theme and concern among academic administrators (Veres, 2016a). Frustration with the processes associated with the operations of a college have academic leaders questioning why they continue to fight for change. The bureaucracy within a college makes it challenging for these leaders to clearly see the connection between the work being performed and the benefit to the student (Taylor, 2014; Veres, 2016b).

Additionally, such an environment makes it challenging for academic leaders to meet the changing employment and educational needs of their students and community (Wallin, 2010). As opposed to a university environment where faculty are strong partners in determining and implementing the educational direction of an institution, the Ontario community-college labor situation is more akin to a trade union environment. This stronger management–worker relationship can create challenges and barriers that consume vast amounts of an academic administrator's time and energy (Veres, 2016b)

Typology of Development Opportunities

When examining the Model of Educational Leader Development, it is useful to explore a typology of development opportunities that provides a useful organizer in terms of the types of learning activities that take place in organizations (Catalfamo, 2009). Schugurensky (2000) clustered learning into three categories of learning: formal, nonformal, and informal.

According to Schugurensky (2000), formal learning is institutionally based; it can take place from preschool to graduate studies. Formal learning is highly institutionalized, or hierarchical, with each level preparing learners for the next level before they are ready to move on. Ministries or departments of education are found at the top of the educational hierarchy with students at the bottom. At the end of the formal learning experience, graduates are usually granted a certificate or a diploma (Schugurensky, 2000). An example of formal leadership development would be achieving a PhD in leadership and policy from Niagara University in Lewiston, New York.

There is strong reason to believe that formal learning is highly valued across the postsecondary system in North America. In 2004, Valeau and Boggs indicated that achievement of a PhD would be a necessity for a senior-level role within an American college (Valeau and Boggs, 2004). When reviewing the college leadership development literature, there is a very strong theme related to the perceived value of formal academic programs (Duvall, 2003; McCarthy, 2003; Skolnik and Giroux, 2001; Valeau and Boggs, 2004). Many postsecondary educators in Canada continue to participate in advanced learning opportunities in PhD and EdD programs offered both in Canada and the United States (Catalfamo, 2009).

According to Schugurensky (2000), nonformal learning refers to learning programs that are organized educational experiences that are external to the formal school system and are typically short-term in duration. There are notable parallels to the formal system, including that there are teachers/instructors or facilitators and there is a curriculum. Nonformal learning, however, is characterized by a higher level of flexibility. Nonformal learning typically does not require a prerequisite, such as the completion of a previous degree, to move into the nonformal learning experience or the completion of one course to move to another course (Schugurensky, 2000).

Nonformal learning does not confer a sanctioned degree, diploma, or certificate licensed by a government body such as a Ministry of Education. An example of this type of nonformal learning would be attending a workshop or conference. There are additional forms of nonformal learning that take place in the workplace, such as the acquisition of knowledge and skills as a function of participation in authentic tasks with support and guidance from others more skilled (Smith, 2003). An example of nonformal leadership development would be learning leadership skills from an appointed workplace coach or mentor.

The final conceptualization within the typology relates to informal learning, perhaps one of the most valuable, yet least recognized, form of learning that takes place in and beyond most workplaces (Schugurensky, 2000). Livingstone (2001) described informal learning as those activities that involve the pursuit of understanding, knowledge, or a skill that occurs without the presence of externally imposed curricular criteria. Informal learning takes place outside of educational institutions with prescribed curriculum and hierarchies.

Most interesting perhaps is the fact that those who engage in informal learning determine the objectives, content, means, and process of acquisition of learning (Livingstone, 2001). For example, an individual who is interested in furthering their understanding of team dynamics may choose to read *Five Dysfunctions of a Team* (Lencioni, 2002) and then reflect on their own leadership style in terms of managing teams within their workplaces. Billet (2001) argued that most learning takes place in informal settings outside the prescribed curricular of formal education.

The Model of Educational Leader Development serves to provide a helpful way to understand the educational leader in terms of motivation, context (work environment), and the development opportunities available to grow the next generation of college leaders. By digging deep and understanding the motivation of aspiring college leaders, those developing and implementing leader-preparation programs can tap into the sense of service and values that drive individuals to pursue leadership roles.

Clearly understanding the environmental factors will help to shape leader development efforts in a more meaningful way. This includes being deeply aware of the bureaucratic nature of the college system, the complexity of the leader role, and the ever-changing needs and demands of college leaders. Developing educational leadership-preparation interventions that make use of formal, nonformal, and informal learning experiences provides emerging leaders with an opportunity to engage in meaningful leadership development that is reflective of the leader's individual needs, as well as the needs of their respective institutions and the broader college system.

DESCRIPTION OF LEADERSHIP DEVELOPMENT PROGRAMS

The challenge of finding, developing, and retaining academic administrators is as prevalent in Ontario as it is in any other jurisdiction. In realizing this, many community colleges in the province have undertaken many unique and different approaches to meet this challenge. The leadership-development programs that are highlighted in this chapter exemplify leader-development approaches that consider the motivating factors of leaders, the environmental context of leaders, and the different types of learning opportunities that grow leaders in an effective way. The four approaches that follow are examples of potential ways of addressing the concern of academic leadership development.

Leadership Capacities Inventory

Colleges often hire passionate and committed faculty and staff that demonstrate a high level of desire to support the institutions and its students. However, postsecondary institutions are not like other businesses; the skills needed to be successful in academic leadership are not always presents in those who wish to the advance into these roles (AACC Leadership Suite, 2013; Boggs, 2011; Burton Jr, 2014; Veres, 2016b). Understanding the uniqueness of the postsecondary environment is essential in finding and developing the *right* leaders to meet these challenges (Bolman and Gallos, 2011).

In recognizing this dilemma, one college has undertaken the creation of a leadership capabilities matrix for both deans and associate deans. The matrix is based on five key pillars that comprise academic leadership: plans for the future, innovates and inspires creativity, influences and cultivates critical relationships, models agility, and develops leadership capacity. These key components are framed in the context of living the values of the institution. For this institution, it is about using their values to guide their actions and decisions, and maintaining a strong focus on the students, staff, and community they serve.

Recognizing that the roles of dean and associate dean are similar, but also unique in many ways, they have developed distinct capability documents for each position. The separate profiles highlight the broader strategic leadership role of the deans, in contrast to the more operationally focus role of the associate deans. The documents also highlight the strong external focus of the deans versus the more internal focus of the associate deans.

The value of these position profiles has been identified in a number of areas at the college. They act as a great reference in the development of academic leadership job postings as well as an excellent tool in the candidate evaluation and interviewing process. By creating a clear understanding of the position responsibilities and abilities needed to accomplish them, these documents aid the college in finding effective academic leaders. Establishing a foundation of core capabilities and promoting a culture of performance, these profiles create a link between the public service nature of the institution and values of the individual.

Demonstrating how these positions speak to the individual's desire to serve (Christensen and Wright, 2011; Greenleaf, 1977; Veres 2016a) creates an alignment between motivation and institutional fit. By clarifying role responsibilities, these profiles also remove the ambiguity that can often be a barrier for attracting quality leaders (Veres, 2016b). Understanding the complexity of the role aids in better preparing individuals for the challenges that they will face (Peretomode, 2012).

In addition to their role in recruitment, the profiles also have a strong utilization in the development of academic leaders. At present, the college uses the position-specific profiles to evaluate the capabilities of an academic leader and create a development plan for their continued support and growth. Although currently only focused on supporting individuals in their present roles, this institution's intention is to investigate how to use these leadership capability profiles in supporting and preparing individuals for future, more senior roles.

This approach to leader development makes use of a nonformal approach to learning. Unlike a formal approach to learning, embedded in educational institutions and providing the learner with a credential that is issued and sanctioned by a governmental body such as a Ministry of Education (Schugurensky, 2000), the use of a position profile is structured in nature and part of an overall process that will lead to learning experiences by way of a developmental plan. The college includes this process as a part of their overall performance-development process; therefore, it lacks the informality of what Livingstone (2001) described as learning that is driven independently by the individual who determines their own objectives, content, means, and process of learning.

Academic Leader Mentorship

Recognizing the uniqueness of the academic leadership environment, it has become apparent that success is often associated with having lived experience in the role. Many senior academic leaders understand the great value for new and emerging leaders to engage with those who have *walked in their shoes* as deans or associate deans. Additionally, they have also identified that one of the great challenges with providing effective mentorship is the availability of mentors. Potential mentors are either too busy with their own responsibilities or so new in their roles that taking on such a responsibility is almost impossible (Veres, 2016b).

One solution that has been identified by a few of the Ontario community colleges is to use recently retired academic leaders as mentors. Mentorship opportunities are an effective tool for enhancing job satisfaction for mentees. Mentees often have a lack of understanding of their roles within the postsecondary environment and are challenged by the bureaucratic nature found in many postsecondary institutions (Boggs, 2003; McPhail Naples, 2006; Valeau and Boggs, 2004). The mentors are often individuals with experience in a variety of academic leadership roles and they themselves have gone through many of the trials and tribulations that new leaders, their mentees, experience (Royer and Latz, 2015).

As often exists with mentoring roles, these relationships take on several forms and functions. New leaders look to these retired deans and associate deans for advice and support. This includes technical guidance on the elements of the position as well as being a sounding board to explore the myriad of challenges they face as educational leaders (Veres, 2016b).

Although the colleges reviewed have implemented mentoring models in different ways to meet their specific needs, there are a few common approaches observed . The nature of the conversations was driven by what the academic administrator felt they needed. The relationships were confidential in nature. The mentor did not provide any formal reporting back to the individual's supervisor nor input into what should discussed.

These mentors took their lead from the mentee and supported the individual in the growth journey. Trust between mentor and mentee was essential to the success of the program. Interestingly, the use of retired academic administrator as mentors was found to promote more trustful relationships as the mentees viewed their mentors as separate from the organization.

One college has taken a different approach by focusing on the use of existing academic leaders as mentors. This approach has its own unique benefits and drawbacks. Although the confidential nature of the relationships is stressed, some mentees are concerned with being fully open and honest with present work colleagues. Also, there is a concern about individuals taking on a mentor role having the time to effectively support the development of their colleague (Veres, 2016b).

To address this environmental barrier, the college has moved to include mentorship as a formal role for those identified leaders and provide them with that recognition within their workload. When provided with the right support and recognition for being a mentor, these types of internally focused matches provide the mentee with a level of current and relevant information that may be missing from a retired individual. Additionally, this approach aides in developing a culture of support and growth within the organization.

In the examples discussed, the mentoring opportunity was presented by the individual's supervisor as an option for consideration. The final decision to be partnered with a mentor was left with the individual. In this way, the academic administrator is given the responsibility to guide their own development. It is an important consideration that delineates this as a developmental opportunity as opposed to performance concern.

The use of a structured mentoring program also utilizes a nonformal approach to learning that is characterized by flexibility for the mentorship partners; yet, there is still a process in place that is designed by the college with expectations and outcomes for the participants. With many mentoring programs, participants are provided with guidelines that include program goal-setting, discussion starters, and ideas for conversation exchanges and shared activities. While mentoring programs often have the "feel" of informality, within the context of the typology described by Schugurensky (2000) and Livingstone (2001), the mentorship programs described in this chapter are nonformal in nature.

Community of Practice

One of the greatest challenges facing new academic administrators is having the time and space to discuss and explore areas of concern and development. Areas of responsibility with academic structures create a variety of related but unique circumstances that each administrator must face. As colleges continue to innovate and diversify their programs, deliveries, and related learning activities, there is no longer a standard or common school year. This reality serves to only heighten the challenge of finding time for collaborative growth and development opportunities.

At one of the colleges, a community of practice was established for the associate deans. The purpose of the group was to create opportunities for the associate deans to discuss concerns and issues in a safe and judgement-free environment. It was through the implementation of a new academic organizational structure that this institution identified the potential need for such a development opportunity. The position of associate dean had just been implemented; there was no formal development infrastructure to support this level of academic leader.

The process used to establish the community of practice and its operating structure were essential components of its success. First, the decision to start the community of practice was one made by the associate deans themselves. Annually, they reflect on their activities and determine if they wish to have the group continue operating. Secondly, they operate in a self-governing manner. Annually, they select one of their members to act as meeting chair and to represent the group with the institution's senior academic leader. They determine the meeting schedule, define and develop their own agendas, and establish their own operating protocols. Because of this, they have been able to establish an environment of trust and a focus on personal and professional development.

An important part of the success of this activity is related to the commitment shown by the institution to support their efforts. Through the endorsement of this activity by the institution's senior academic leader, the associate deans can access college resources to aid in their development and signal the importance of this to the rest of the college. Individual deans each work to create the space in associate deans' schedules to allow their involvement to occur. Communicating this level of organizational commitment aids in establishing a trusting and supportive environment (Kumar and Giri, 2009; Veres, 2016b).

The associate deans meet six times a year and are supported by one of the institution's academic leaders. The selected individual is endorsed by the group to ensure there is a level of trust that allows for open and honest discussion to occur. This individual acts as a resource for the group, managing logistical requirements of their meetings and acquiring the needed resources for the group to meet their established purpose. Resources often come in the form of speakers and content specific experts from across a variety of college departments. Another key role that they play is to ensure the meetings are not used for operational or college informational purposes.

The environment established for this community of practice allows for several positive outcomes to occur. By sharing approaches, the associate deans support each other in identifying opportunities for improved processes and efficiencies. As these academic administrative roles often work in an element of isolation, the opportunity to meet collectively allows for informal support networks to form and engage beyond just the meetings. The discussions that occur often bring to light policy and procedural concerns that can then be addressed through the appropriate institutional process.

Communities of practice tend to be very organic in nature; the evolution of this community of practice demonstrates this characteristic. It has grown to be another example of a nonformal learning experience. It is supported by the college, there is structure to the process, there are predetermined topics, including guest speakers offering knowledge-sharing on a variety of topics, and there is a facilitator appointed at the regular meetings. While there is collective self-determination of the learning that takes place, participants are not left to their own devices to pursue independent exploration of learning which would be characteristic of informal learning (Billet, 2001; Livingstone, 2001).

Integrated Organizational Development Model

Academic institutions often develop and/or create access to opportunities that support the growth of academic administrators. These can be in response to an identified need or as a more proactive approach to professional development. In some cases, institutions will even create a suite of opportunities that support their leaders. When layered with a culture of learning, this integrated approach to the development of academic administrators can be a powerful tool in recruiting, developing, and retaining great leaders. Such an approach can be a model for other institutions to follow.

One college has not only established an extensive and integrated approach to leader development but has done so in parallel with the emergence of a culture of learning and growth. As part of an institutional review, it was identified that there was neither a planned approach to leader development nor the necessary resources to develop and implement such an approach. This review led the senior leaders of the institution establishing a *Centre for People and Development*. This decision then allowed for the creation of an integrated approach to leader development that touched on many facets of what academic administrators needed.

One component of the opportunities provided focused on the technical knowledge needed to be successful in a community college environment. As with many postsecondary institutions, there are often knowledge areas that are unique to their sector or their institution. As many new academic administrators begin their roles with limited academic leadership experience, the ability to gain such technical knowledge quickly and easily can help them establish a level of confidence and effectiveness in performing their duties. These workshops are focused on topics such as human resource practices, union contracts, related legislation, and financial processes.

A second component offered centers on leadership and interpersonal elements of the role. This component takes the form of a *leadership institute* that related groups of leaders take over the course of a year. This institute involves a series of nonformal learning opportunities that aids in the development of the individual's decision making, communication, conflict resolution, and change management skills. These activities are framed around an understanding of self. This focus places an emphasis on the importance of learning who one is as a leader, so one can effectively support the vision, mission, values, and direction of the organization.

The final element of this integrated approach is the opportunity to access mentoring and coaching resources. Individuals who take on an academic administrative position not only come in to those roles with variety backgrounds and experiences, but also progress and grow in different ways. The provision of these one-to-one development opportunities provides the leader with a way of personalizing their development path in a way that best meets their needs.

To create a culture of learning, an institution must be continually looking for ways to support and celebrate their efforts. When institutions support and celebrate the development of their leaders, individuals are more likely to engage in leadership development activities. Organizations that foster a culture of learning are viewed to have supportive and progressive work environments (Veres, 2016b). At this college, the senior leadership teams have provided resourcing for leadership development and have also been actively involved in the learning experiences as participants. They bring an understanding of the uniqueness of the community college environment (Bolman and Gallos, 2011; Eddy, 2012) and they also model the importance of establishing a culture that embraces change (Brown, Martinez, and Daniel, 2002; Cloud, 2010).

The first group to participate in the *leadership institute* was the college's senior team. Through their experience, they grew as leaders and developed an understanding of the value of the activities that the next level of leaders would experience. This reinforced their support and advocacy for the leadership-development process at their institution. The senior leadership team continues to challenge the *Centre for People and Development* to look for new ways to support and celebrate organizational leaders, and to expand the reach of its programs to potential emerging leaders.

The integrated approach to leadership development utilized at this institution is an excellent example of a leadership-development program that is very comprehensive, tapping into a variety of nonformal learning experiences to help leaders develop and grow over time.

The first phase of the program provides essentials of knowledge for new leaders by way of workshops. The curriculum is clearly laid out with a facilitator and each participant is provided with a baseline of knowledge critical for leaders in the college system. The second phase of the program also uses nonformal learning. It is a structured learning process that takes leaders through a journey of self-discovery, exploring nontechnical skills that are essential in their roles as college leaders. Finally, the third phase of the program, mentoring and coaching, is carefully crafted by the institution to continue the professional development of the leader using a more individualized approach.

All phases of the program are coordinated, managed, and overseen by the institution. While there is little doubt that individuals are encouraged to explore informal learning within the context of this program, the framework of the program is, in fact, nonformal.

SUMMARY AND CONCLUSION

Postsecondary leadership is not like that of any other of business. To understand and embrace its uniqueness is necessary for success (Bolman and Gallos, 2011). Within this environment, the Ontario community-college system provides for its own unique situation that creates the opportunity for its own creative solutions. Throughout this chapter we have highlighted four such solutions that have aided in meeting the challenge of finding, developing, inspiring, and retaining quality leaders.

The Model of Educational Leader Development presented in figure 4.1 shows the integrated nature of educational leader development. Understanding what motivates individuals to take on such roles, there is a connection to public service motivation and the concept of servant leadership. Creating an environment that minimizes bureaucratic processes and promotes a culture of learning sets the stage for leader development. And finally, by providing nonformal development opportunities, leaders are given the tools to support not only their growth but also sustain success of the institution.

REFERENCES

American Association of Community Colleges (AACC) Leadership Suite. (2013). *AACC competencies for community college leaders*. Washington, D.C.: American Association of Community Colleges. http://www.aacc.nche.edu/newsevents/Events/leadershipsuite/Documents/AACC_Core_Competencies_web.pdf.

Anderfurhren-Biget, S., Varone, F., Giauque, D., and Ritz, A. (2010). Motivating employees of the public sector: Does public service motivation matter? *International Public Management Journal, 13*(3), 213–46. doi:10.1080/10967494.2010.503783.

Bass, B. M. (1985). Leadership: Good, better, best. *Organizational dynamics, 13*(3), 26–40.

Billet, S. (2001, November). *Participation and continuity at work: A critique of current workplace learning discourses*. Paper presented at the Joint Network/SKOPE/TLRP International workshop Context, power, and perspective: Confronting the challenges to improving attainment in learning at work, University College of Northampton, England. http://www.infed.org/archives/e-texts/billett_workplace_learning.htm.

Boggs, G. R. (2003). Leadership for the twenty-first century. In W. E. Piland and D. B. Wolf (Eds.), *Help wanted: Preparing community college leaders in a new century* (pp. 15–25). San Francisco, CA: Jossey-Bass.

Boggs, G. R. (2011). Community colleges in the spotlight and under the microscope. *New Directions for Community Colleges, 156*, 3–22.

Bolman, L. G., and Gallos, J. V. (2011). *Reframing academic leadership*. San Francisco, CA: Jossey-Bass.

Boroski, E., Buchsbaum Grief, T. (2009). Servant-leaders in community colleges: Their values, beliefs, and implications. *Review of Business Research, 9*(4), 113–20.

Bright, L. (2011, Spring). Does public service motivation affect the occupation choices of public employees? *Public Personnel Management, 40*(1), 11–24.

Bright, L. (2013). Where does public sector motivation count the most in government work environments? A preliminary empirical investigation and hypotheses. *Public Personnel Management, 42*(1), 5–26. doi:10.1177/0091026013484575.

Brown, L., Martinez, M., and Daniel, D. (2002). Community college leadership preparation: Needs, perceptions, and recommendations. *Community College Review, 30*(1), 45–73.

Burton Jr, V. S. (2014). How to be a successful administrator. *Journal of Contemporary Criminal Justice, 30*(4), 409–26.

Catalfamo, H. (2009). *An examination of leadership development within Ontario's colleges: Building personal, interpersonal, and organizational capacity.* Unpublished doctoral dissertation. University of Toronto, Toronto, Canada.

Cejda, B. D., and Leist, J. (2013, Fall). Voices from the field: Learning about community college transformation and change from the words of practicitioners. *Journal of Applied Research in the Community College, 21*(1), 15–24.

Christensen, R. K., and Wright, B. E. (2011). The effect of public service motivation on job choice decisions: Disentangling the contributions of person-organization fit and person-job fit. *Journal of Public Administration Research and Theory, 21*(4), 723–43. doi:10.1093/jopart/muq085.

Cloud, R. C. (2010, Spring). Epilogue: Change leadership and leadership development. *New Directions for Community Colleges, 149*, 73–79.

College Administrator. (2009). Leadership development: As baby boomers near retirement, how do colleges develop tomorrow's leaders? College Administrator.

College Employer Council, and OPSEU. (2014, October 23). Collective bargaining. http://www.thecouncil.on.ca/.

Cooper, J., and Pagotto, L. (2003). Developing community college faculty as leaders. In W. E. Piland and D. B. Wolf (Eds.), *Help wanted: Preparing community college leaders in a new century* (pp. 27–37). San Francisco, CA: Jossey-Bass.

Day, J. (2015). Illinois Community College administrators' views regarding the present retirement crisis in the community college system: A descriptive study. *Liberal Arts, 19*(2), 3–12.

de Guzman, A. B., and Hapan, M. F. (2013). It takes two to tango: Phenomenologizing collaborative mindset of Filipino academic deans. *The Asia-Pacific Education Researcher, 22*(3), 315–26. doi:10.1007/s40299-012-0056-7.

Dennison, J. D., and Levin, J. S. (1989). Responsiveness and renewal in Canada's community colleges: A study of change in organizations. *The Canadian Journal of Higher Education, 14*(2), 41–57.

Duvall, B. (2003). Role of universities in leadership development. In W. E. Piland and D. B. Wolf (Eds.), *Help wanted: Preparing community college leaders in a new century* (pp. 63–71). San Francisco, CA: Jossey-Bass.

Eddy, P. L. (2012). A holistic perspective of leadership competencies. *New Directions For Community Colleges, 159*, 29–39. doi:10.1002/cc.20024.

Greenleaf, R. K. (1977). *Servant leadership: A journey into the nature of legitimate power and greatness.* New York, NY: Paulist Press.

Gregory Stone, A., Russell, R. F., and Patterson, K. (2004). Transformational versus servant leadership: A difference in leader focus. *Leadership and Organization Development Journal, 25*(4), 349–61. doi:10.1108/01437730410538671.

Herzberg, F. (1982). *The managerial choice: To be efficient and to be human* (2nd ed.). Salt Lake City, UT: Olympus.

June, A. W. (2013). How administrators measure their success. *The Chronicle of Higher Education, 59*(43). https://www.chronicle.com/article/How-Administrators-Measure/140419.

Kumar, B. P., and Giri, V. N. (2009). Examining the relationship of organizational communication and job satisfaction in Indian organizations. *Journal of Creative Communications, 4*(3), 177–84.

Leist, J., and Travis, J. E. (2013). Community college leadership: Advancing by degrees. *Journal of Applied Research in the Community College, 21*(1), 37–41.

Lencioni, P. (2002). *The FIVE dysfunctions of a TEAM.* San Francisco, CA: Jossey-Bass.

Levin, J. S. (1999). Missions and structures: Bringing clarity to perceptions about globalization and higher education in Canada. *Higher Education, 37*(4), 377–99.

Livingstone, D. W. (2001). *Adults' informal learning: Definitions, findings, gaps and future research.* Ontario, Canada: Centre for the Study of Education and Work. https://tspace.library.utoronto.ca/bitstream/1807/2735/2/21adultsinformallearning.pdf.

McCarthy, C. (2003). Learning on the job: Moving from faculty to administration. In W. E. Piland and D. B. Wolf (Eds.), *Help wanted: Preparing community college leaders in a new century* (pp. 39–49). San Francisco, CA: Jossey-Bass.

McPhail Naples, F. (2006). *Aspirations of community college leadership: A study of talent engagement and the barriers and motivation for faculty leadership development.* Doctoral dissertation. http://ezproxy.niagara.edu/login?url=?url=https://search-proquest.com.ezproxy.niagara.edu/docview/305371533?accountid=28213.

Moynihan, D. P., and Pandey, S. K. (2007, January/February). The role of organizations in fostering public service motivation. *Public Administration Review, 67*(1), 40–53.

Palmer, D. J. (2013). College administrators as public servants. *Public Administration Review, 73*(3), 441–51. doi:10.1111/puar.12037.

Peretomode, O. (2012, June). Work and stress among academic administrators of higher education institutions in Delta state. *European Scientific Journal, 8*(13), 29–46.

Perry, J. L., and Hondeghem, A. (2008). Building theory and empirical evidence about public service motivation. *International Public Management Journal, 11*(1), 3–12. doi:10.1080/10967490801887673.

Piland, W. E., and Wolf, D. B. (2003). In-house leadership development: Placing the colleges squarely in the middle. In W. E. Piland and D. B. Wolf (Eds.), *Help wanted: Preparing community college leaders in a new century* (pp. 93–100). San Francisco, CA: Jossey-Bass.

Polonsky, G. (2003). *Moving educational leaders from implicit to explicit leadership: An action research study.* Unpublished doctoral dissertation. University of Toronto, Toronto, Canada.

Purkey, W. W., and Siegel, B. L. (2003). *Becoming an invitational leader: A new approach to professional and personal success.* Atlanta, GA: Bumbry Holdings.

Royer, D. W., and Latz, A. O. (2015). Community college leadership transition through the framework of appreciative inquiry. *Community College Journal of Research and Practice, 40*(8), 1–12. doi:10.1080/10668926.2015.1072594.

Savage-Austin, A. R., and Honeycutt, A. (2011, January). Servant leadership: A phenomenological study of practices, experiences, organizational effectiveness, and barriers. *Journal of Business and Economics Research, 9*(1), 49–54.

Schugurensky, D. (2000). *The forms of informal learning: Towards a conceptualization of the field.* Toronto, Canada: Centre for the Study of Education and Work. https://tspace.library.utoronto.ca/bitstream/1807/2733/2/19formsofinformal.pdf.

Skolnik, M. (2002). *From the 1960s to the 2000s: Reflections on the difficulty of maintaining balance between the university's economic and non-economic objectives in periods when its economic role is highly valued.* A paper prepared for a symposium in celebration of the 175th Anniversary of the University of Toronto Charter. 1–15.

Skolnik, M., and Giroux, R. (2001). Advancing learning-centered education at the state or provincial level. *Leadership Abstracts, 4*(4), 1–3.

Smith, P. J. (2003). Workplace learning and flexible delivery. *Review of Educational Research, 73*(1), 53–88.

Taylor, J. (2014). Public service motivation, relational job design, and job satisfaction in local government, *Public Administration, 92*(4), 902–18. doi:10.1111/j.1467-9299.2012.02108.x.

Valeau, E. J., and Boggs, G. (2004). An assessment of the association of California community college administrators mentor program. *Community College Review, 31*(4), 48–61.

Veres, D. (2015, May). *Attracting and retaining great leaders: What motivates academic administrators.* Winnipeg, Canada: Colleges and Institutes Canada Conference.

Veres, D. (2016a). Job satisfaction of Ontario college academic administrators. Unpublished data.

Veres, D. (2016b). *A phenomenological understanding of the experience of academic administrators: Motivation, satisfaction, retention, and succession planning.* Doctoral dissertation. Retrieved from: ProQuest Dissertations Publishing, 2016. 10156423.

Wallin, D. L. (2010, Spring). Looking to the future: Change leaders for tomorrow's community colleges. *New Directions for Community Colleges, 149,* 5–12.

Wheeler, D. (2012). *Servant leadership for higher education.* San Francisco, CA: Jossey-Bass.

White, G. W. (2013). First-year experiences of associate deans: A qualitative, multi-institutional study. *Research in Higher Education Journal, 22*(1), 1–29.

Wright, B. E. (2007, January-February). Public service motivation: Does mission matter? *American Society of Public Administration, 67*(1), 54–64.

Yukl, G. (2010). *Leadership in organizations* (7th ed.). Upper Saddle River, NJ: Prentice Hall.

About the Authors

Matt Byrne is associate dean (primary education) in the School of Education at Edith Cowan University in Perth, Western Australia. His current research involves exploring how education and health can work together in disadvantaged contexts.

Holly Catalfamo is professor of human resources at Niagara College, Niagara-on-the-Lake, Ontario, Canada. The recipient of the Gold Leadership Excellence Award from Colleges and Institutes Canada (2017–2018), Dr. Catalfamo has contributed to the development of educational institutions within Ontario and across the globe. Dr. Catalfamo's research interests are in the areas of leadership development, global capacity building through education, and gender equity.

Tak Cheung Chan is professor emeritus of educational leadership, Kennesaw State University, Georgia, and a graduate of the University of Georgia. He was a classroom teacher, assistant school principal, school principal, and district office administrator. His research interests include educational planning, facility planning, school business administration, school finance, and international education.

Dehau Liu is professor of education of the College of Education Science, Hunan Normal University, Changsha, Hunan Province, China. He specializes in curriculum development and implementation. As senior faculty, Dr. Liu took the lead in many research initiatives of his college by sharing his unique professional experiences in science education and elementary-education reforms.

Hamit Özen is assistant professor in the Educational Sciences Department at Eskisehir Osmangazi University, and a graduate of Eskişehir Osmangazi University of Turkey. His research interests include educational leadership and critical pedagogy.

Andy Scott is responsible for school and system leadership programs offered by International School Leadership, based in Ontario, Canada. In addition, he has led school and system leadership-development projects in Denmark, Sweden, Jordan, Peru, and Abu Dhabi.

Zhiding Shu is dean of the School of Education, Huzhou Normal University, Huzhou, Zhejiang Province, China. His previous experience includes chairing the Center of Educational Leadership at Shanghai Normal University and the Center of Teacher Training at Zhejiang Normal University, China. Dr. Shu's research interests include educational leadership, teacher education, and educational philosophy.

Selahattin Turan is professor in the Educational Sciences Department at Uludağ University of Turkey, and a graduate of The Ohio University in the United States. His research interests include applied behavioral sciences and leadership theory and practice.

David Veres is adjunct professor in the Leadership and Policy PhD program at Niagara University, Lewiston, New York. With over twenty years of academic leadership roles in the Ontario Community College system, Dr. Veres's scholarly interests are in the areas of policy development, leadership, and strategic planning.

About the Editor

Peter R. Litchka is professor of educational leadership at Loyola University Maryland, where he has been since 2006. Prior to coming to Loyola, Peter was in public education for thirty-three years, including being a classroom teacher, a school and district administrator, and twice a superintendent of schools in New York state. He is author/coauthor of three books in educational leadership, numerous scholarly articles, and has presented in the United States as well as in Canada, Cyprus, Israel, Poland, and Turkey. Peter received his bachelor's degree from the State University of New York at Geneseo, his master's degree from Johns Hopkins University, and his doctorate from Seton Hall University. He is currently president of the International Society for Educational Planning.

Other books by Peter R. Litchka:

The Dark Side of Educational Leadership: Superintendents and the Professional Victim Syndrome (with Walter Polka, 2008)
Living on the Horns of Dilemmas: Superintendents, Politics and Decision-Making (with Walter Polka and Frank Calzi, 2014)
Exemplary Leadership Practices: Learning from the Past to Enhance Future School Leadership (2016)

www.ingramcontent.com/pod-product-compliance
Lightning Source LLC
Chambersburg PA
CBHW021215240426
43672CB00026B/316